UNIX® Curses Explained

The author and publisher of this book have used their best efforts in preparing this book. These efforts include the development, research, and testing of the theories and programs to determine their effectiveness. The author and publisher make no warranty of any kind, expressed or implied, with regard to these programs or the documentation contained in this book. The author and publisher shall not be liable in any event for incidental or consequential damages in connection with, or arising out of, the furnishings, performance, or use of these programs.

UNIX® Curses Explained

Berny Goodheart

PRENTICE HALL

New York   London   Toronto   Sydney   Tokyo   Singapore

This book was typeset by the author. UNIX programs formatted the text and printed the final copy.

Cover design: from an original painting "Haiti & The Philipines" by James H. Evans

Printed in Australia by Impact Printing, Brunswick, Vic.

2345 94 93 92 91

ISBN 0 13 931957 3

National Library of Australia Cataloguing-in-Publication Data

Goodheart, Berny
  UNIX Curses Explained.

  Includes index
  ISBN 0 13 931957 3

  1. UNIX System V (Computer operating system) I. Title

005.43

Library of Congress Cataloguing-in-Publication Data

Goodheart, Berny
  UNIX Curses Explained / Berny Goodheart.
    p. ISBN 0-13-931957-3 cm.
  Includes bibliographical references and index.
  1. UNIX (Computer operating system) I. Title.
QA76.76.063G663 1990   90-7820
005.4'3--dc20   CIP

Prentice Hall, Inc., *Englewood Cliffs, New Jersey*
Prentice Hall Canada, Inc., *Toronto*
Prentice Hall Hispanoamericana, S.A., *Mexico*
Prentice Hall of India Private Ltd, *New Delhi*
Prentice Hall International, Inc., *London*
Prentice Hall of Japan, Inc., *Tokyo*
Prentice Hall of Southeast Asia Pty Ltd, *Singapore*
Editora Prentice Hall do Brasil Ltda, *Rio de Janeiro*

 PRENTICE HALL

A division of Simon & Schuster

To my wife Peppy

and the children Natalie, Benjamin and Melisah

for being extremely patient

A special dedication to:

Warren Simon (NEC Information Systems) without whom this book would never have been possible, Marcus Bain (Olivetti UK) who has been both a brother and friend, Martin Sullivan and Paul Gundry who gave birth to my career and my man Peter Lloyd (the Bengal Tiger) of TANDEM Computers Incorporated.

To all the staff at Prentice Hall Australia: I am indebted to Andrew Binnie (Senior Editor) for giving me the inspiration (and being a good drinking partner). Gratitude beyond measure goes to Gillian Gillett (Senior Production Editor) who helped me turn my best effort into a better one. A very special thank you to Ian MacArthur (Production Manager), Janet Cooke (Assistant to Senior Editor), Terry Dodd (Assistant to Senior Editor), Chris Richardson (Assistant to Senior Editor) and Kate Ormston-Jeffrey (Freelance Editor).

I would also like to thank those who spent their precious time reviewing this book: Associate Professor John Lions (Department of Computer Science, The University of New South Wales), Greg Rose (Technical Director, Softway Pty Ltd) and Michael John an old-time UNIX hack who spent many hours helping me put it together.

Finally, a special hello to my Mum, and Dad (get yer hair cut !).

CONTENTS

PREFACE

Originally, *curses* was developed at the University of California at Berkeley, and became a standard part of their version of UNIX known as the Berkeley Software Distribution (BSD), currently 4BSD.

Many vendors license *curses* and other packages like the *vi* editor from Berkeley, and include it with their version of UNIX as extensions to their release, often referred to as Berkeley enhancements.

It all started in the late 1970s when Bill Joy, in writing his editor *ex* (probably more famous by the name *vi* nowadays), wrote a set of routines which read a terminal capability database. The database, then named *termcap*, generally described how to manipulate individual terminals and what they where capable of. The routines he created, which accessed the *termcap* database, implemented optimal cursor movement.

Kenneth C.R.C. Arnold took these routines almost without changes and derived from them what is known today as the **curses package**.

The *curses* package has since undergone many changes, and is probably more sophisticated than Bill Joy could ever have imagined when he first thought of the idea.

Today the *curses* package is still evolving. Mark Horton created a version distributed with AT&T System V, known as **AT&T Curses**. The database, named **terminfo**, now uses binary files which provide a more efficient method of retrieving terminal capabilities.

The new *curses* package provides even more capabilities, with even more routines, and support for yet more terminals. It now includes support for alternate character sets and color, with even better optimization. Who knows what the future of the UNIX *curses* packages will provide?

UNIX was originally designed as a development system. You only have to look at the wealth of routines provided with the operating system to aid the development of new projects. Although UNIX was not originally designed as the result of any corporate strategy, its main place today is in commercial institutions, with even more complex processors at the heart of the operating system.

Because of the growth in the technology of what was once known as **dumb terminals**, into what are now becoming terminals with as much complexity as the hardware that controls them, and at even more affordable prices, it has become quite apparent to UNIX programmers how important it is to have a standard library of routines to work with when writing an application which manipulates a terminal screen. Even more important, the library must provide terminal independence and a clean easy-to-work-with interface. It should take all the hard, dirty work out of gaining information from a terminal description database. Indeed, the library should hide this task, but provide it, if necessary. The library should be portable and should follow a standard that can adapt to future enhancements. The UNIX *curses* package provides this standard and provides an interface that is both complete and easy to use, with nearly as much ease as is necessary to simply print and read things to and from a terminal.

The look and feel of a program and how well it sells lies in the way it interacts with the user. Everybody knows that first impressions mean more than any other aspect when it comes to gaining some interest from a prospective client.

Nowadays we see windowing systems constantly creeping into the UNIX scene — The X Window System, NeWS and Open Look, for example. However, these systems are still a minority, so the ASCII video terminal as we know it still dominates the UNIX market.

But we still create programs that are line oriented. Why is this?

The answer lies in a program's complexity. This is not to say that every program needs to use a facility such as *curses*. But rather it is better to ask the question, why isn't there an easier way to write a program that uses the full capabilities of the terminal? Fortunately with UNIX there is a better way: the answer is to use *curses*.

This book provides the internal knowledge needed to write *curses*-based programs using the C Programming Language on the UNIX Operating System. It also covers the art of creating *terminfo* database descriptions.

A basic knowledge of the C Language and an understanding of constructs such as pointers, data structures, arrays and so on is assumed. However, because the book is instructive, it is not necessary for the reader to be familiar with the UNIX operating system, although it would help in understanding the philosophy of the subject.

This book has been laid out to serve two purposes: one is to provide a reference text on the subject, the other is to provide a tutorial description which will supply enough knowledge for an already competent C programmer to create *curses* or *terminfo*-based programs.

Throughout the book UNIX System V Release 3 has been used as the basis for discussion and as the source for specific examples. Information in the book which is defined as being specific to another particular version of UNIX is identified throughout the text. Where one system differs from another I have tried to provide enough information to outline those differences.

As an aid to both student and professional, a reference manual is provided as part of this book. It has been laid out in a similar fashion to the standard UNIX documentation. While studying the text the reader is encouraged to refer to this manual.

This book was created (after many sleepless nights) using a macro package *tmac.bk* written by myself together with a C program which created the index. It was produced on a Siemens PT10 laser printer using **nawk, grap, pic, tbl, eqn** and **ditroff** under UNIX System V.3. The macro package and the index-making program are available to all budding authors.

Finally, the manual pages provided in the reference section of this book are available separately on magnetic media. They are supplied in nroff(2) source form and packed using the public domain compress utility. They are also available in the standard UNIX pack(1) form.

Over the past years my experience of writing programs under UNIX has inevitably led me to use the *curses* package many times over. Unfortunately, the *curses* documentation is sparse, and good documentation for *curses* is hard to come by; I have had to learn the hard way. This book will, I hope, remove most of the problems I had to tackle, and prepare you for designing an application using the standard UNIX *curses* package.

CHAPTER 1

Understanding windows

An understanding of *curses* is vital for any C programmer writing interactive screen-based programs under UNIX. The programs you write should be totally independent of whatever type of terminal the target program will run on. The *curses* library provides a set of over 200 routines that enable you to manipulate a terminal screen regardless of what type of terminal you are using.

To master these routines you need to understand the *curses* data structure known as a WINDOW, since almost all the *curses* routines manipulate this structure in some way. Once you have read this chapter and understood exactly what a window is, you will be well on your way to understanding the rest of the book.

1.1 What is a window?

A window is an internal data representation of an image of what a particular rectangular section of the terminal display may look like. The terminal display as a whole could be said to be a window, its dimensions defined by its outermost extremities, those being the sides of the cathode ray tube.

That said, we could then say that a window with the dimensions of one character in length and one character in height is in fact a window of the size of one character. This is the smallest window that *curses* could possibly handle, but a window could also have the dimensions of 128 characters in length and 50 characters in height. Unfortunately this would be bigger than the size of most terminals, but in theory, anyway, it is a window.

A *curses* window is not a physical entity. It is only a data representation of how you would like a rectangular portion of the physical screen to look. A window is a preallocated resource stored in the machine's memory. As you manipulate it, nothing actually happens to the physical screen until you are ready to update it. When you are ready, you use the *curses* function wrefresh() to update the physical screen. This overwrites or superimposes the internal window on the physical screen.

Curses provides a default window which represents your terminal screen. Its size is defined by the dimensions of the terminal screen your *curses* program is to work with. *Curses* allows you to manipulate several windows individually, or all at the same time. It also allows windows to contain windows within themselves, known as sub-windows. You can create as many windows as you want; the only limitation is the amount of memory available which your program can use.

The philosophy behind *curses* is really quite simple. You can work with the default window provided by *curses*, or you can create your own window or windows. You may choose to use both methods; you can use the default window provided, as well as create and work with your own. Either way, *curses* does not care.

1.2 The *curses* window

The *curses* internal representation of a window is defined in the data structure:

```
struct _win_st.
```

This structure is defined in the **/usr/include/curses.h** include file and is typedefed WINDOW.

Since there have been many different versions of *curses*, this structure is bound to vary between different versions of UNIX. In practice, however, the structure is common to most systems, except perhaps for some additional flags or changes in types.

The WINDOW structure below is taken from a UNIX System V.2 version of *curses*, but to get a true picture of the window structure on your system, now is a good time to print it out.

```
struct _win_st {
        short  _cury, _curx;
        short  _maxy, _maxx;
        short  _begy, _begx;
        short  _flags;
        chtype _attrs;
        bool   _clear;
        bool   _leave;
        bool   _scroll;
        bool   _use_idl;
        bool   _use_keypad;
        bool   _use_meta;
        bool   _nodelay;
        chtype **_y;
        short  *_firstch;
        short  *_lastch;
        short  _tmarg,_bmarg;
};

typedef struct _win_st WINDOW;
extern WINDOW *stdscr, *curscr;
```

Buried somewhere among all the `#ifdefs` and `#ifndefs` in the `<curses.h>` file you will find the definition of the above *curses* data structure. Incidentally, if you have printed this out, you may have noticed that the first line of code in the file is indeed an `ifndef`:

```
#ifndef WINDOW
```

The corresponding `#endif` is at the bottom of the file. This is useful if you are administering multiple source files. If `WINDOW` has already been defined and you inadvertently try to include the `<curses.h>` file again within your program, the C preprocessor will ignore anything between.

This structure is in fact *curses'* internal representation of a window. It contains all the necessary data and information which *curses* needs to manage the window on the terminal screen. For *curses*, anything inside or belonging to a window is modifiable. Anything outside a window is undefined and in most cases illegal as far as *curses* is concerned. Even if you simply want to print some text on the screen, *curses* requires you to place the desired text into a window. It is important to realize that almost all the *curses* routines totally depend on this window structure.

It is equally important to realize that, although a window structure is an internal representation of a *curses* window, it may not necessarily bear any relation to what is really being displayed on the terminal screen. The window structure is used solely to hold data and information which describes a window, and is used to build a potential image of a portion of the true terminal screen. You should think of it as a buffer area set aside to represent a portion of the screen (or indeed the whole screen) which you can modify by using the routines provided in the *curses* library.

1.3 The terminal screen

Before *curses* can manage your terminal screen it needs to know what it looks like. When *curses* starts up, the first thing it does is clear the screen. It then places the cursor in the *home* position, which is the top left-hand corner of the screen. *Curses* then knows exactly what your physical screen looks like and where the cursor is situated.

Curses also needs to know how you, the programmer, would like it to look. For this reason, *curses* provides two WINDOW data structures, `curscr` and `stdscr`.

The `curscr` window holds a data representation of what is currently displayed on the real terminal screen, and the `stdscr` window is provided as a default window for you to work with. You can manipulate the `stdscr` window within your program. When you want the terminal screen to look like the `stdscr` window, you issue a `refresh()` call to update the `curscr` window, which in turn makes the terminal screen look like the `stdscr` window.

An important thing to remember here is that it is not good practice to access the `curscr` window directly. Changes should be made only to the appropriate window you are working on, and then, by calling `wrefresh()` on that window, you can instruct *curses* to update the `curscr` window for you internally. You should treat the `curscr` window as a reserved window for the private use of the *curses* routines only.

If you wish, you can maintain several different ideas of what a portion of the terminal screen is to look like. You do this by maintaining several windows, with each window maintaining its own private WINDOW data structure. Changes to the windows can be done in any order at your discretion. You can update the real terminal screen at will simply by calling `wrefresh()` on the particular window that you want the terminal to display. The *curses* package will do all the hard work for you, relieving you of the worry about which is the best way to accomplish the task.

1.4 Window structure variables

The WINDOW structure contains all the necessary information to enable *curses* to update the terminal screen optimally. By keeping state information about a particular window inside its WINDOW data structure, *curses* can obtain the relevant information it needs to carry out its instructions. For example, it needs to know how big the window is, and whereabouts on the terminal screen it is to be placed. In fact, all the information *curses* requires to maintain a window is contained within the WINDOW data structure.

Understanding this data structure is essential for learning how to use *curses*. For this reason we will start by learning the information that is contained within it and what purpose each variable has. As mentioned previously, there are many versions of *curses* spanning many versions of UNIX; there is even a version of *curses* which runs under MS-DOS. Consequently, there are many versions of this data structure also. Therefore we will concentrate on the necessary variables (the universal ones) which will be important to us while writing *curses* programs.

Curses programs which make direct reference to these WINDOW structure variables are inherently non-portable. For this reason *in-line* code examples are not given within the following variable explanations, as they may be inappropriate for your installation. It is sufficient that you understand what *curses* needs them for. As long as you use the interface provided, that is, the library of routines which make up the *curses* package, your programs will be portable.

So, what are these variables? The variables `_cury` and `_curx` contain the current y,x coordinates of the cursor on the window. If characters are added to the window, this is where the next character is to be inserted. Note that the given coordinates are in the y,x order and not the conventional x,y order. This is how the *curses* routines use them, and if this sounds a bit confusing, it will all become clear as you read on.

To specify the location of a windows cursor, you need to use a coordinate system. *Curses* uses a coordinate system consisting of horizontal and vertical axes at right angles to each other. The coordinates are numbers that define the location of a point within a given window with reference to an origin. The coordinates themselves are equally spaced units in both **Y** (vertical) and **X** (horizontal) directions. Y coordinates are expressed in terms of lines (or rows) down the screen, and X coordinates are expressed in terms of columns (or character positions) across it.

The Y coordinate is the vertical position within a *curses* window, and its origin is the top left-hand side of the window. The X coordinate is the horizontal position across a *curses* window, its origin also being the top left-hand side. Both Y and X origins are 0 (zero)-based. If, for example, we are dealing with window coordinates of 0,0 this refers to the top left-hand corner of the window. This is referred to as the **home** position.

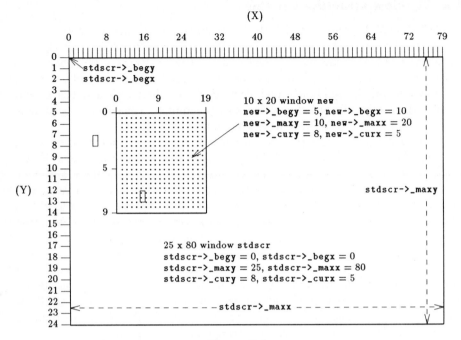

Figure 1.1

The variables _maxy and _maxx specify the outermost dimensions of a *curses* window.   _maxy specifies how many lines span down the window.   Similarly, _maxx specifies how many columns span across it.

The variables _begy and _begx specify the starting y,x coordinates of the window.   From these variables *curses* can compute the position of the window in relation to the dimensions of stdscr. However, the upper left-hand corners of a window are always 0,0 even if the window is placed in the center of the terminal display.

Figure 1.1 shows a terminal display with a user-created window named new. This window is 10 lines in height and 20 columns in width. The new window is placed on top of stdscr at coordinates _begy = 5, _begx = 10. Also, in both windows the cursor is moved to line 8, column 5 within their respective window areas.   From this diagram you can see how *curses* sees the window and what its coordinates are in relation to stdscr, which are in most cases the dimensions of the true terminal screen.   Since many terminals are 25 lines high by 80 columns wide, we will assume for this example that this is the size of our terminal screen.

The _flags variable is used as a bit mask. Many *curses* routines manipulate this bit mask, or at least consult its contents throughout program execution. Generally, the _flags variable is used for optimization purposes.   The following is a description of what the various flags are:

_SUBWIN   This tells *curses* that the window is a sub-window (see Section 4.11).

_ENDLINE   This tells *curses* that the right-most end of each line in the window is the edge of the screen.

_FULLWIN   This tells *curses* that the window is the size of the physical screen; that is, the window fills the whole terminal screen.

_SCROLLWIN   This tells *curses* that the terminal will scroll if a character is placed into the lower right edge of the physical screen. Although present in System V versions of *curses*, it is not used.

_FLUSH   This flag is currently unused.

_ISPAD   This tells *curses* that the window is a pad; basically this means the window can be bigger than the physical terminal screen. This is explained in depth later.

_STANDOUT   This tells *curses* that characters added to the screen are to be displayed in *standout* mode. This means characters added to the window will be highlighted in some way, normally reverse video. This flag is provided for compatibility reasons only. It has now been replaced by the constant A_STANDOUT.

_NOCHANGE   Used for optimization purposes. When refreshing a window, and if a line on the window has not been changed since the last update on the window, *curses* assumes that there is no need to update it again and so ignores it.

_WINCHANGED   This tells *curses* that the window has been modified in some way since it was last updated.

_WINMOVED   This tells *curses* that the cursor has been relocated to another position within a window. When next reading input into the window, the window is refreshed first so that the cursor is in the correct position for the read.

Some of the following flags may also be implemented on your version of UNIX, but these are no longer available with System V.

_FULLINE   Tells *curses* that each line on the window is the full width of the screen.

_INSL   Tells *curses* if a line has been inserted into the window.

_DELL   Tells *curses* if a line has been deleted from the window.

All these flags are manipulated internally by the *curses* routines. For portability reasons it is bad practice to manipulate these flags yourself within your *curses* program. The *curses* library provides routines that do this for you.

The _attrs variable contains various attribute flags relative to a window. Attributes are specified as associated video display capabilities of a terminal. Not all terminals support them.

Various *curses* routines are used to turn attributes on and off in a window. For example, you may want to display a string of characters on the screen in say, highlighted video mode. By simply turning the *standout* video attribute on, any characters added to the screen will be added with this attribute, provided of course the terminal is capable of displaying them in this way. For example, this call to wattron() tells *curses* to turn on *underline* mode for the window named mywin:

```
wattron(mywin,A_UNDERLINE);
```

Any characters now added to mywin will be underlined. Internally, the function wattron() uses the C logical operator "|" to OR in the specified attributes into the _attrs variable. In this case A_UNDERLINE would have been OR'ed in. Thus the code for wattron() would look something like this:

```
wattron(win, attrs)
WINDOW *win;
int attrs;
{
    return(win->_attrs |= attrs);
}
```

Curses is clever enough to figure out which attributes are set by examining the _attrs flag. If attributes are set they are automatically OR'ed into characters as they are added to the window. The package applies these attributes to the terminal screen when refresh() is called on the window. For example, let us say that we want to display a string of characters in *standout* mode. As *curses* updates the physical screen, and finds that the next character is to be displayed in this mode, it sends a special escape sequence to the terminal which, hopefully, renders the terminal in *standout* mode. If *curses* finds that the next character to display is in normal display mode and *standout* mode is current, it will send the escape sequence to turn *standout* mode off.

Several display attributes may be supported. For example, *blink* mode and *underline* mode are supported in the newer versions of *curses*, but once again you will have to check what attributes have been defined in your <curses.h>

file. It is also worth pointing out here that, even if a desired attribute is supported on your system, if the terminal you are using does not support it then obviously it will not be applied. Even if the terminal does support it, the terminal capability database *terminfo* must be configured to enable *curses* to realize this feature (see Chapter 7). If *curses* finds that it can't apply an attribute to a window for any reason, it just ignores the instruction to apply it.

The `_clear` variable is used within *curses* to specify whether to clear the terminal screen before the next call to `refresh()`. The first time `refresh()` is called, this variable is set to TRUE. It is important to realize that if this variable is TRUE, then the clear screen sequence is sent to the terminal screen and the screen will be cleared irrespective of the physical size of the window involved. So it can be seen that this variable is significant only for windows that are the full size of the terminal screen. You can set or clear this flag with the `clearok()` function. Thus, to force *curses* to clear the screen entirely before redrawing it again, you would do the following:

```
clearok(stdscr,TRUE);
refresh();
```

The `_leave` variable is used to tell *curses* to leave the cursor where it was before the `refresh()` was issued. Once again, you can set or clear this flag with the `leaveok()` function:

```
leaveok(stdscr,TRUE);
```

This function is useful if you are writing a program which is not affected by where the cursor is left. Leaving the cursor where it is placed after an update reduces the amount of motion needed to move the cursor around the screen, so fewer characters are transmitted to the terminal. However, if `_leave` is set, then `refresh()` may place the cursor at an undefined place on the terminal screen after the update is done. *Curses* assumes that leaving the cursor in some undefined place is undesirable, so it tries to make the cursor invisible when it is in this mode.

The `_tmarg` and `_bmarg` variables contain the top and bottom margins of the scrolling region within a window. If the window is allowed to scroll, the amount scrolled will be the area between and including the lines specified by `_tmarg` and `_bmarg`. These variables are used by the `scroll()` function which scrolls a window up a line.

The `_scroll` variable tells *curses* if the window is allowed to scroll or not. This is set or cleared in a similar way with the `scrollok()` function. The following example tells *curses* that scrolling is allowed in the `stdscr` window:

```
scrollok(stdscr,TRUE);
```

If scrolling is enabled, the window will scroll whenever an attempt is made to move out of the scrolling region. This can be achieved in many ways, and writing to the lower right-hand corner of the window, or typing new-line while the current line is the bottom line in the window are the most common examples. It is also possible to make a window scroll illegally if you force *curses* to move out of its defined area.

The _use_idl variable tells *curses* to use the terminals insert/delete line feature, if the terminal is capable. You can set or clear this flag with the idlok() function. The insert/delete line mode tends to be visually annoying but it is often required for screen scrolling. For this reason *curses* by default supplies all windows with this flag disabled, but under UNIX System V.3 *curses* manages the insert/delete line feature differently; an extra WINDOW structure variable is used — _need_idl. *Curses* uses this variable to keep track of when the insert/delete line facility was last used. By doing this *curses* can use the insert/delete feature only if it is really necessary, which is more efficient. So, under UNIX System V.3, windows are supplied with this mode enabled.

The _use_keypad variable tells *curses* to use the keypad. If the keyboard does not have a keypad, then *curses* will ignore this variable. The *keypad* is the set of keys on the terminal keyboard which perform some sort of action. For example, the arrow keys and function keys form part of the keypad. By default *curses* disables the keypad and does not treat these keys specially. If, however, the keypad is enabled, then the *curses* input routine wgetch() returns a value which corresponds to a set of defined constants in the <curses.h> include file. These constants have symbolic names which relate to these keys: that is, the defined constant KEY_HOME corresponds to the key on the keyboard marked "home". If the keypad is disabled then wgetch() will return the next character in the character sequence produced by the key. To enable or disable the keypad, you use the function keypad(), which tells *curses* whether to treat sequences of characters generated by the keys on the keypad specially.

The _use_meta variable is used to tell *curses* if it is to operate in *meta* mode. If _use_meta is enabled, characters returned by wgetch() are not stripped of the eighth bit, which is the normal default mode. This mode is useful for terminals which support a *meta shift key*, typically used to select a non-text character set. On UNIX systems prior to System V this can only be achieved by setting the terminal into *raw* mode.

Eight-bit processing is not necessarily a very good idea. Many applications use only seven bits, especially if used over a network. If anything between the terminal and the application strips the top bit, eight-bit processing is impossible. Not all UNIX systems can do eight-bit processing, although this is often due to a deficiency in the system's terminal device driver. The function meta() is used to enable or disable *meta* mode:

```
meta(stdscr,TRUE);
```

The _nodelay variable tells the input routine wgetch() to return without delay if there are no characters waiting in the input queue. This is useful if you do not want the terminal to hang, waiting for keyboard input. This mode is by default disabled, and the function nodelay() is used to set or clear the _nodelay flag. This example turns delay mode off in window mywin. When wgetch() is next called on this window it will return without hanging, also wgetch() will return −1.

```
nodelay(mywin,TRUE);
```

The _y variable is of most interest to us, since this is the two-dimensional array of pointers to lines containing characters that we manipulate in a window. _y[n] is the nth line, and _y[n][j] is the jth character on the nth line. The array's size is defined by the *curses* initialization routines newwin() and newterm(). The effective declaration of the array for the window stdscr can be better seen like thus:

```
_y[LINES][COLS];
```

You may have noticed that this variable is defined with a storage class of chtype. This is usually typedefed to an unsigned char, but the size depends on your implementation of *curses*. Generally, the more attributes your *curses* package handles, the bigger it has to be. This type is not configurable unless of course you have a source code license, in which case you will be able to re-compile the *curses* package and add new attributes (this is not recommended). Almost all the routines which add or delete characters from a window manipulate this array in some way.

The _firstch and _lastch arrays are to help *curses* optimize the number of characters on a window it is to update. Both these arrays have an element for every line in a window. Certain *curses* routines such as wrefresh() test these arrays to find out if a line has changed in any way since last being updated. Their purpose is to tell *curses* where to start and finish working on each line within the window when refresh() is called, thus helping *curses* optimize the number of characters on the window which need updating on the terminal screen. For example, the *curses* routine touchwin() is used to touch every character in a window, therefore making *curses* think the whole window has been changed. In fact none of the characters are changed on the window at all. The routine simply sets every _firstch element to 0, which tells *curses* to start updating from the beginning of each line. Then every _lastch element is set to the width of the window, which tells *curses* to end updating at the end of each line. Basically this forces *curses* to think that every character position in the window has been changed and needs updating on the physical screen. Thus the function touchwin() would look something like this:

```
touchwin(win)
WINDOW *win;
{
     register x;

     for(x = 0; x < win->_maxy; x++) {
          win->_firstch[x] = 0;
          win->_lastch[x] = (win->_maxx - 1);
     }
}
```

Now, when refresh() is called on the *touched* window, it tests the contents of these arrays to find out where on each line it is to begin and end updating.

We have now covered all the variables in the WINDOW data structure. However, as mentioned earlier, you may have some extra variables in this data structure on your system, and some systems may not even have some of the variables mentioned here, although we have covered all the variables we need to know about when writing a *curses* program. But be warned, these variables should *never* be accessed directly within your *curses* program. The *curses* package provides you with a comprehensive library of routines which do this in a controlled way. If you do access these variables directly, your programs may not be portable. If at some time in the future you want to port your *curses* program to another UNIX system, the window structure on that implementation may differ from the one that the program was originally written on.

CHAPTER 2

The curses working environment

Before we go any further, we need to learn what *curses* requires of its environment before a program will work properly. This chapter explains these requirements in detail. It also explains what *terminfo* is, and compares it with the old system *termcap*. Other topics covered are how *curses* and *terminfo* work together, and what other UNIX utilities are provided with the *curses* package. Finally, we will learn how to compile and run a *curses* program.

2.1 Terminal basics

Oddly enough, the standard terminal device driver on UNIX provides no support for modern-day terminals. In fact, UNIX still treats a terminal like the old hardcopy daisywheel printer type of terminals we used to use like the Qume 5 or the Diablo 1620.

Generally, UNIX does not support mice, bit-mapped screens, or graphic workstations, although some of these devices are starting to appear in the high end of the UNIX marketplace. Companies such as Sun Microsystems and Hewlett Packard can now provide UNIX workstations that support high-resolution bit-mapped displays with **look and point** graphics-based interfaces. These interfaces provide a mouse-driven windowing environment which allows you to run several processes in parallel, each in their own separate window on the terminal display. However, most of us are not fortunate enough to work in these environments and are forced to use CRT terminal devices such as the Wyse 50.

All interaction between the user and the UNIX operating system is handled by an asynchronous terminal connected through some port. The normal standard communication method used for these devices is RS-232. But we will not go into any great detail about RS-232, as there are many texts already available on the subject. It is sufficient to say that this standard provides a method by which data can be transmitted by the terminal's keyboard and received by the computer. Similarly, the computer can transmit data to the terminal which is then displayed on the screen.

The only way UNIX knows about a particular device is through a piece of software linked into the kernel called a device driver. A device driver provides a platform by which a program can read from and write to a device through system entry points provided in the way of C function calls, called **system calls**.

Basically, these system calls are subroutines built within the UNIX kernel, but UNIX adopts a unique approach to devices. Each device is represented by a special file which exists in the file system along with other ordinary files and directories. User programs can interact with a device controlled by a particular driver by associating themselves with these special files (see Figure 2.1). For example, programs running on the system console are associated with the special file /dev/console, but a program running on the console can open another device, thereby associating itself with that device also. Depending on how the device driver implements its user interface, user programs can control the way the driver is to operate. For example, the **stty** command allows you to modify how the terminal driver operates. The command **stty 300** tells the driver to set its operating speed to 300 baud; once the driver receives this command, it will operate in this mode.

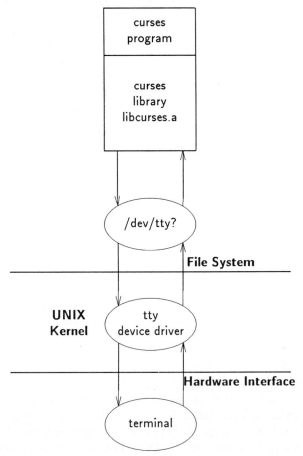

Figure 2.1: *Structure of the UNIX device interface*

The *tty* (a historical UNIX term for a teletype terminal) device driver essentially controls the data path between the computer and the terminal. However, although a program may have some control over a terminal through this device driver, it has no conception of what sort of terminal it is controlling. Let us take a look at what is involved in controlling the terminal.

The keyboard contains a set of alphanumeric keys which generate codes for the different letters, numbers and symbols as defined by the American Standard Code for Information Interchange (better known as ASCII). If a key is pressed on the keyboard an ASCII character code is generated and sent to the computer. The device driver controlling the port to which the terminal is connected receives the character and then proceeds to echo it back to the terminal so that it can be displayed. This assumes, of course, that the terminal is operating in full-duplex mode. At the same time, the character is placed into the internal system character input buffers so that a process using the read(2) system call on this device is able to read it.

On the terminal, as each character is received it is placed on the screen next to the last character that was received, and so on, until it comes to the edge of the terminal screen, in which case the terminal normally starts a new line below the last one displayed. However, for some codes received by the terminal, the terminal performs some sort of action instead of displaying the character. For example, if you type a **Control-G** (ASCII BEL) at the keyboard, the terminal usually sounds a beep (or bell) when it receives the character from the computer. Similarly, if you enter a carriage return, the terminal normally moves the cursor to the beginning of the next line to emulate a typewriter carriage return.

Codes which tell the terminal to perform some sort of action are called **control codes**. The problem is that each terminal responds differently to them. A **Control-L**, for example, will clear the screen on a Datamedia 1520, but on a Televideo 925 it makes the cursor shift to the next column position without destroying the character under it.

The question is, how do we write a program that controls a terminal if we do not know what sort of terminal we are dealing with? We could hard-code our program with device-dependent control codes to control a particular terminal we may know about, but what happens if someone with a different terminal runs our program?

This question was faced by Bill Joy when he was creating his editor *vi*. He came up with the idea of creating a database of terminal descriptions, outlining each individual terminal's capabilities. He also created a set of functions which could read this database to figure out how to control the terminal it was working with. Those routines were taken by Ken Arnold, and he created the *curses* package. Although it has gone through many changes since then, this is the only package currently available on UNIX which can provide some means of managing ASCII based terminals, regardless of what type they are.

2.2 Terminfo

The term *terminfo* refers to a group of routines which are built into the *curses* library and use the capabilities of a terminal. Terminfo also refers to a database of binary files, with each file describing an individual terminal's capabilities. Normally when we mention terminfo, we are referring to the latter.

The terminfo database, as shipped with UNIX System V, contains descriptions for over 150 different terminals which can be used with *curses* written applications, and it is growing rapidly with every new release of the operating system.

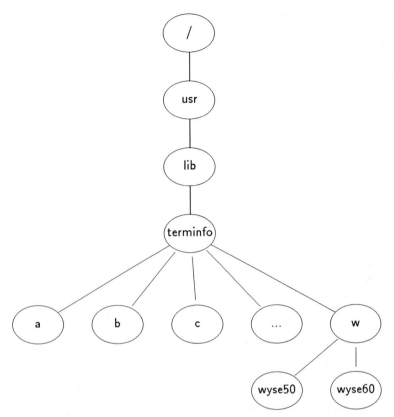

Figure 2.2: *Example of the terminfo database structure*

A terminfo description specifies what a particular terminal can do and what steps
are needed to perform certain operations on the physical screen. For example,
the description will specify how many lines and columns a terminal has; whether
to use X-on/X-off handshaking; if the terminal is capable of displaying in reverse
video; what function keys the terminal has; what special control codes are
required to move the cursor around the screen; and so on (see Chapter 7). The
terminfo database is a set of compiled files, with each file describing an
individual terminal.

   These files are referred to as **terminfo description files** and are normally
found in a directory under `/usr/lib/terminfo` (see Figure 2.2). They are
compiled from text-based files. Each directory under this has a single character
name, which is the first character of the terminal's name. Take, for example, the
Wyse 50 terminal: its terminfo description file would normally have a full path
name of `/usr/lib/terminfo/w/wyse50`.

The reason I say 'normally' is because it is possible to have your own version of a terminfo database, as you will see later when we discuss how to write terminfo description source files.

As we learned earlier, terminfo also refers to a set of functions which form part of the *curses* library. These functions are low-level routines which *curses* itself is built upon. They are provided for programmers who want to access the terminal directly without using the *curses*-based screen management functions. For example, if your terminal supports programmable function keys, there are certain low-level terminfo routines which can help you program them without having to use *curses*.

For *curses* to work properly, it has to be able to search the terminfo database to find the description file containing information about the terminal.

2.3 The *curses* environment

Before *curses* can search the terminfo database for your terminal type, it needs to know what its name is. This is achieved by assigning the terminal's name to the environment variable **TERM**.

You can do this by defining this variable in your **.profile** if you use the **Bourne** or **Korn** shell, or your **.login** if you use the **Berkeley C shell**. You can also set this variable on the command line. To do this using the Bourne shell, you enter the following:

                    TERM=wyse50 ; export TERM

If you are using the Berkeley **csh**, then you enter the following:

                    setenv TERM wyse50

Of course, these examples assume that your terminal is a Wyse 50.

It is also a good idea to initialize the terminal properly before using it. This is done with the command **tput init**. (Note: the **init** argument to **tput** is not available with UNIX System V.2.) This should also be placed in your **.profile**, after specifying **TERM**. **Tput** consults the terminfo database using the low-level terminfo routines. If it finds that the terminal has to be initialized, it extracts the necessary initialization sequences and then sends them to the terminal.

When you start up a *curses* or terminfo-based program, the terminfo database is scanned until it finds an entry matching that which is specified in your shell environment variable: **TERM**. In the above example, which uses the Wyse 50, the file `/usr/lib/terminfo/w/wyse50` would have satisfied the search.

In the unlikely case of your terminal having no terminfo description file defined, you may have to obtain one from somewhere or build one for it. Before you go to the trouble of writing your own terminal description, it is worth contacting the manufacturers of the terminal and asking them if they have one, or at least a client who has built one. In any case, most modern terminals can emulate another make of terminal, so check your terminal's documentation first. One final point: if you have to write your own description file, don't start from scratch. There is bound to be a terminal description in the terminfo database that is close to describing your terminal; with the command *infocmp* you can uncompile a terminfo file and use the output as a template for creating your own. The method of writing your own terminfo description file is discussed in Chapter 7.

Curses does make use of other environment variables, but unlike the **TERM** environment variable, they are not mandatory. If you have the environment variable **TERMINFO** defined, *curses* will use a **local** terminfo description database directory instead of the default /usr/lib/terminfo directory. For example, if you want terminfo to search for a terminfo description using your own private database, you can do this by entering the following:

```
TERMINFO=${HOME}/myterminfo ; export TERMINFO
```

In this case terminfo will use the directory myterminfo in your home directory to search for descriptions. This facility is useful for developing and testing new description files, and also when you don't have permission to modify the /usr/lib/terminfo directory itself.

There are two terminfo variables set in each description file. These are **lines** and **cols**. They tell *curses* the physical dimensions of the terminal's screen. You can override these values by setting the variables **LINES** and **COLUMNS** in your shell environment.

You can experiment with these variables by using the UNIX utilities **pg**, **more** or **vi**. These programs use *curses*; changing the value of these variables will affect the way they interact with the terminal. Try paging through a long text file with **pg**. If you set the variable **LINES** to, say, 10, notice the way **pg** gives you 10 lines at a time to view instead of the normal full screen of lines.

To set this variable enter the following at the command line:

```
LINES=10 ; export LINES
```

2.4 The /etc/ttytype file

Some UNIX systems which use *termcap* use this file to assign a particular terminal type to a specified serial port. This is almost always true for some early versions of UNIX System V, XENIX and 4BSD based systems. However, on later versions of UNIX System V this file is generally used by the *tset* command. The /etc/ttytype file contains a single line per configured port. Each line has two fields separated by white space; the first field is a terminal type name (as listed in *termcap*) which will be used by the *tset* and *login* programs to assign a default terminal type to the shell environment variable **TERM**. The second field is the

name of a serial port (as listed in /dev) which the terminal is connected to. For
example:

```
wy50    tty01
ansi    tty02
vt100   tty03
```

2.5 The /etc/ttys file

The *init* program uses the information in the /etc/ttys file to activate the serial
ports. The file contains a single line per port. Each line describes how the
terminal is to be configured. For example:

```
1ttty01
1ttty02
1ttty03
```

The first character on each line is either 1 or 0 (zero) depending on what action
is to be taken by *init*. If it is 1, then *init* will enable the line for logins by placing
a *getty* on the port. If it is 0 (zero), then *init* will ignore the line and the port is
disabled.

   The second character's meaning can differ between systems. On UNIX
System V and 4BSD based systems it specifies the baud rate. The *getty* program
looks up this character in an internal table to find the baud rate. Some systems
use this character to indicate a process which *getty* will spawn instead of *login*.
The rest of the line specifies the name of the port (as listed in /dev) to
configure.

   Note: the format of the /etc/ttys file is different on BSD 4.3 versions of
UNIX. Also, the /etc/ttytype file is not used. However, the information from the
/etc/ttytype file is incorporated in the /etc/ttys file. Here is an example:

```
tty01   "/usr/etc/getty std.9600"    vt100       on    # Warren
tty02   "/usr/etc/getty std.9600"    vt100       off   # Marcus
tty03   "/usr/etc/getty d2400"       dialup      on    # 890-5544
ttyH0   "/usr/etc/getty std.9600"    plugboard   on    # Berny
ttyp0   none                         network            # pseudo-tty
```

The first (tty01) line will allow users to login at 9600 baud with a terminal type
of vt100. On the second line (tty02) the fourth field is specified as "off"
therefore this line is disabled. The third line (tty03) is configured for use with a
modem running at 2400 baud. The fourth line (ttyH0) is connected to a plug-
board which allows terminal cables to be patched via a multiplexor. The last line
(ttyp0) is set up for network use which uses the *pseudo-ttys* and so *getty* is not
enabled. Note that any text placed after the pound '#' is ignored — it is used for

comments.

Note that later versions of UNIX System V use */etc/inittab* and do not use */etc/ttys.*

2.6 Other *curses* utilities

The *curses*/terminfo package abounds with useful utilities. Not all implementations have them, but here is a list of what may be available on your system:

captoinfo   A utility for converting the *termcap* database into terminfo description source format.

infocmp   A tool for printing and comparing compiled terminfo descriptions.

tic   A terminfo description file compiler.

untic   A tool for printing and comparing compiled terminfo descriptions (pre-System V.3).

tabs   A tool for setting non-standard tab stops.

tput   A tool for outputting individual terminal capabilities.

tset   This program is primarily used to initialize or reset the terminal but it is also used to configure the **TERM** shell environment variable.

2.7 Termcap

Back in the good old days (i.e., pre-System V), *curses* used a single text file for its terminal description database. The file was named **/etc/termcap** (some Berkeley distributions used **/etc/btermcap**), and all the routines that did the low-level work were placed in a separate library appropriately named **termlib**.

Unfortunately, the termcap file grew larger as each new terminal description was added to it. This became a bit of a problem to the termlib routines, as it took longer and longer to search for a terminal description within this file. And so terminfo eventuated.

Termcap is now no longer supported, although some OEMs have decided to supply both systems with their release of UNIX because some programmers have teething problems using the new terminfo system.

Basically, each system is used in the same way, using the same environment variables. The exception is the **TERMINFO** variable which now replaces the old environment variable **TERMCAP**, although essentially it functions the same way.

Each new terminal description was added to the termcap file as it became available.

Of course, the new terminfo system uses a set of individual compiled *binary* description files (one for each terminal type), instead of a single *text* file. A special compiler called **tic** (Terminal Information Compiler) was developed. For each new terminal description a text file was created and compiled using **tic**, the output of which is in binary form. During the design of terminfo, many new capabilities were added, and the whole process of searching for a terminal description became more efficient.

The introduction of terminfo forced a major re-engineering of *curses*. Many new, more powerful functions have been added to the *curses*/terminfo library. To maintain compatibility to programs written for earlier versions of *curses*, all the old low-level termcap/termlib functions are simply emulated using the newer terminfo routines (see Chapter 9). Although these routines are still supported, they may eventually be phased out in future versions of UNIX.

By the way, if you are using a pre-System V version of UNIX (i.e., the termcap version), you can speed up *curses* by placing the most commonly used terminal descriptions at the top of the **/etc/termcap** file. This will help speed up termcap searching algorithms.

The following list describes the routines that are now obsolete, or have been replaced:

`crmode()`	replaced by `cbreak()`.
`fixterm()`	replaced by `reset_prog_mode()`.
`gettmode()`	now a dummy no-op function.
`nocrmode()`	replaced by `nocbreak()`.
`resetterm()`	replaced by `reset_shell_mode()`.
`saveterm()`	replaced by `def_prog_mode()`.
`setterm()`	replaced by `setupterm()`.

2.8 Cursor optimization

The *curses* library provides cursor optimization, but what does cursor optimization mean?

Most ASCII-based terminal screens are 80 columns wide by 25 lines high. That's a total of 2000 characters! What's more, an extra byte per screen character used to hold video attributes is usually required; this makes a total of 4000 bytes of data in all. If *curses* had to transmit 4000 bytes of data to the terminal every time the screen was to be refreshed, response time would lengthen considerably, not to mention the extra overload that would be placed on the system. For this reason *curses* updates only the parts of the terminal screen which really need updating. It does not waste time by refreshing every character on the screen. If a part of the screen has not been changed since the screen was last refreshed, *curses* ignores it. This means that the amount of data transmitted to the terminal is kept to a minimum. This method of being able to optimize the amount of characters transmitted to the terminal is called: *cursor optimization.*

2.9 *Curses* **programming requirements**

When you write a *curses* program, you need to include the header file <curses.h> in your source file. This header file contains many global and external variables and definitions used by a *curses* program. This include file is the subject of our next chapter, so we will not go into any detail here.

2.10 **Compiling your program**

Your *curses* program is just another C program. You compile it just as you would compile any other C program under UNIX, except that you need to include the *curses* library **/usr/lib/libcurses.a**. You do this by instructing the link editor to search for this library at compile time. This is achieved by using the -**l** (that's a lower case L, not the number one) option to the **cc** command. If you are using the old **termcap/termlib** version of *curses*, you may have to link in the **/usr/lib/libtermlib.a** library also. For example, to compile the program **foo.c** you enter at the command line:

> **cc -o foo foo.c -lcurses**

If you are using the old *termlib* version of *curses*, you enter:

> **cc -o foo foo.c -lcurses -ltermlib**

If you still have problems compiling your *curses* program on a pre-System V version of UNIX, try substituting -**lcurses** with -**ltermcap**. If all goes well, your source program **foo.c** will produce an executable file called **foo**.

2.11 **Run-time complications**

If your program *dumps core* (a UNIX term for the process by which the UNIX system dumps a core-image-file of the process in the current working directory, caused by the program executing an illegal instruction), make sure you have placed the initscr() function in your source code before any other *curses* function call. Also, make sure that you are not using delwin() to inadvertently free up windows that don't exist.

If the program runs, but leaves the terminal in a funny state when the program returns to the shell, check that you have called endwin() before exiting the program. You can usually fix the terminal by typing one of the following sequences:

ˆJ stty sane ˆJ *or* **ˆJ reset ˆJ** *or* **tput reset**

The sequence **ˆJ** is typed by holding down the control key while at the same time pressing the key labeled **J**. If this does not fix the terminal, you have really confused the *tty* driver — try logging out and logging back in again. If this fails, you may be able to fix the problem by killing the login shell from another terminal.

If your terminal messes up when you run your program, or it does not respond as you expected it to, make sure that the terminal's terminfo description is correct.

You may get the following message on the screen during program start-up:

```
Sorry, I don't know anything about your "FooBar" terminal.
```

This means that *curses* can't find the terminfo description for your terminal type. In the example message above, **TERM** is set to **FooBar**; in practice it would be set to the name of your terminal. Make sure that the **TERM** environment variable is set to reflect your current terminal type.

Some systems continue to support the old termcap system, but maintain the new terminfo system as well. This may cause complications at compile time. The best solution is to refer to the documentation provided with your system. Such systems may have two header files for *curses*, with the termcap system using <ocurses.h>, and the terminfo system using <curses.h>. If this is the case with your installation, you may be trying to link the wrong *curses* library to your program. Try replacing **-lcurses** with **-locurses** as an option to **cc** on the command line. One way of finding out the name of the *curses* library on your system is to grep the output of ls in /lib or /usr/lib using **curs** as the search string:

ls /lib /usr/lib | grep curs

There is a bug inherent in some System V.2 releases of *curses* if nodelay() is used. The program returns EOF to the calling process on termination. If the calling process being used is the login shell, you get logged off the system. The fix is to call nodelay(stdscr,FALSE) just before calling endwin() in the exiting stages of your *curses* program.

Finally, *curses* takes full control of the terminal that it is running on. If you want to do any special I/O, the *curses* package provides routines that will do it for you. This means that you should not use the stdio package directly. If you try to do anything outside *curses'* control, it may leave your terminal in an unpredictable state.

CHAPTER 3

The <curses.h> Include file

The *curses* package is still evolving, with almost every new version of UNIX providing some change to the package. Consequently, these changes have also affected the <curses.h> include file.

This next chapter discusses the various variables and definitions you may find in this header file, and what differences you may find between various releases of the package.

3.1 Function return values

Almost all *curses* functions return a status value. This facility is normally used to test whether a function has succeeded with its operation or not.

For *curses* functions which return a *boolean* value, the constants OK and ERR are defined in the `<curses.h>` header file. If one of these functions encounters an error during its execution, then ERR is returned; similarly, the constant OK is returned if everything went okay.

If a *curses* function returns a pointer of some sort, then the relevant pointer type will be returned if the function completed its operation without an error. If an error does occur, the value returned will be (*type* *)NULL, where *type* is the defined base type.

For example, the function `newwin()` is used to create a new window. If the window is created successfully, `newwin()` returns a pointer to it. However, if `newwin()` fails for some reason, then (WINDOW *)NULL is returned. We can see how to test for this return value in the following example:

```
WINDOW *new;

initscr();
win = newwin(0,0,0,0);

if( win == (WINDOW *)NULL ) {
    endwin();
    printf("could not allocate new window\n");
    exit(1);
}
```

In this example, if `newwin()` fails it will return (WINDOW *)NULL and the program exits. Notice that `endwin()` is called before exiting the program. This tells *curses* to set the terminal driver back into an *out-of-curses* mode. If this is not done, then the program will exit leaving the terminal in an unpredictable state. For example, if echo is turned off with `noecho()`, the terminal is likely to be left in no-echo *(half-duplex)* mode.

3.2 Other include files

The `<curses.h>` file automatically includes `<stdio.h>`. Also, on UNIX System V, `<termio.h>` is included. If you are running a BSD or XENIX system, then `<sgtty.h>` is included.

On System V, `<unctrl.h>` is also included in `<curses.h>`. This file contains a macro function, `unctrl()`. This is used to extract a printable version of an ASCII character. Passing the value 7, which is a control G to `unctrl()`, will return the string "^G".

Since <curses.h> automatically includes these header files, there is no point in including them again within your source file. Although harmless to do so, it is wasteful and prolongs compile time.

3.3 Terminal dimensions

The variables LINES and COLS specify the height and width dimensions of the terminal screen. These variables are also defined in <curses.h>. Initially they have no value. You can set them within your *curses* program if you wish, but this may render your program useless on a terminal which has dimensions different from those you have specified. It is highly recommended that you let *curses* figure out how many lines and columns the terminal has.

The dimensions of a terminal are described by the variables *lines* and *cols* in the terminfo description file. When you start up a *curses* program with initscr(), this information is assigned to the variables LINES and COLS respectively. However, if you have defined **LINES** and or **COLUMNS** in your shell environment, their values will be used instead.

For example, if you are logged on to the system over a modem line running at a slow baud rate, say 300 baud, it is a good idea to set the LINES variable so that a *curses*-based program will use a smaller working area on the screen. This saves you having to wait for the whole screen to be updated at 300 baud every time the screen is refreshed. Incidentally, you don't have to do this for *vi* since *vi* automatically resets the size of the working window anyway, depending on the current baud rate.

On the system I use, this variable has been implemented within the /etc/profile script so that it is automatically set at login time:

```
#! /bin/sh
#
# test the tty port for slow baud rate
#
stty | grep 9600 2>&1 > /dev/null
if [ $? = 0 ]
then
    LINES=10 ; export LINES
fi
```

3.4 The stdscr and curscr windows

The external variables stdscr and curscr defined in <curses.h> are two virtual-window pointers. These windows are initially the size of your terminal screen and are created by the *curses* start-up function initscr(). The stdscr window is provided for you to work with, while the curscr window is generally reserved for internal *curses* use.

curscr knows what your terminal looks like, while stdscr is how you, the programmer, would like it to look. The curscr window represents your terminal screen. Every time you refresh a window, *curses* copies the changed portions of that window onto it and updates the physical screen contents.

3.5 Pseudo-functions for stdscr

Curses provides many functions which are specifically set up to deal with the stdscr window. For example, to get character input from stdscr, you use the function getch(). If you want to get character input from another window, you use wgetch(). In fact getch() is not a function at all, it is a pseudo-function (or macro) defined in <curses.h>. Here is what the definition of getch() looks like:

```
#define getch()  wgetch(stdscr)
```

Function names are consistently prefixed with w when they are applied to a specific window. Such functions have at least one parameter, the window you want the function to operate on. For example, wgetch() is prefixed with a w and is said to be window-specific.

Almost all functions that are set up for stdscr are in fact pseudo-functions defined in <curses.h>. They are made up of real functions and, sometimes, other pseudo-functions. We can demonstrate this by writing our own pseudo-function called addctrlch(), which is also specific to stdscr. This routine adds a printable version of a character to the stdscr window:

```
#define addctrlch(ch) addstr(unctrl(ch))
```

The interesting thing about addctrlch() is that it is solely made up of other pseudo-functions. Let's take a step back and have a look at addstr():

```
#define addstr(str) waddstr(stdscr, str)
```

addstr() is also a pseudo-function; its purpose is to add a string of characters to stdscr. What about unctrl() ?

```
#define unctrl(ch) (_unctrl[(unsigned) ch])
```

This pseudo-function extracts an entry from the array of strings in _unctrl[] (defined in <unctrl.h>) and ch is used to index this array.

From this example you can see how *curses* uses pseudo-functions for stdscr. However, this is just an example. In fact, *curses* never puts non-printable characters on the screen — it parses each character with unctrl() first, anyway. If you try to add a non-printable ASCII character (say, a Control-

G) to a window, *curses* produces a printable version of it (see Table 3.1). In this case, Control-G would be printed as **^G** on the screen. So, this pseudo-function is pointless, but it serves a purpose for this example.

Table 3.1

unctrl[] STRINGS							
00 ^@	01 ^A	02 ^B	03 ^C	04 ^D	05 ^E	06 ^F	07 ^G
08 ^H	09 ^I	0a ^J	0b ^K	0c ^L	0d ^M	0e ^N	0f ^O
10 ^P	11 ^Q	12 ^R	13 ^S	14 ^T	15 ^U	16 ^V	17 ^W
18 ^X	19 ^Y	1a ^Z	1b ^[	1c ^\	1d ^]	1e ^^	1f ^_
20	21 !	22 "	23 #	24 $	25 %	26 &	27 '
28 (	29)	2a *	2b +	2c ,	2d -	2e .	2f /
30 0	31 1	32 2	33 3	34 4	35 5	36 6	37 7
38 8	39 9	3a :	3b ;	3c <	3d =	3e >	3f ?
40 @	41 A	42 B	43 C	44 D	45 E	46 F	47 G
48 H	49 I	4a J	4b K	4c L	4d M	4e N	4f O
50 P	51 Q	52 R	53 S	54 T	55 U	56 V	57 W
58 X	59 Y	5a Z	5b [	5c \	5d]	5e ^	5f _
60 `	61 a	62 b	63 c	64 d	65 e	66 f	67 g
68 h	69 i	6a j	6b k	6c l	6d m	6e n	6f o
70 p	71 q	72 r	73 s	74 t	75 u	76 v	77 w
78 x	79 y	7a z	7b {	7c		7d }	7e ~	7f ^?

3.6 Moving around the screen

To move the cursor to a specified location within a window, use the function `wmove(win, y, x)`. The parameters `y` and `x` are the offset coordinates of *line* and *column* in the window. Let us say that we want to add a string at window coordinates y = 10 and x = 5. Our code would look something like this:

```
wmove(win,10,5);
waddstr(win,"Hello World");
wrefresh(win);
```

There are a few points to outline here. First of all, notice how consistent the parameter `win` is throughout each function call. In fact, this is so for all functions that are prefixed with `w`. Notice also the call to `wrefresh()`. This function should be called so that the physical screen update takes place. If we don't call `wrefresh()`, nothing will be displayed on the screen.

The `<curses.h>` include file also defines a set of pseudo-functions for moving around a window. These pseudo-functions are prefixed with `mv`, and require at least two arguments, `y` and `x`, which specify the coordinates to move to. If a function has both prefixes ala `mvw`, then it requires at least three arguments — the window, y and x, and they must be specified in that order. Here is what the definition for the pseudo-function `mvwaddstr()` looks like:

```
#define mvwaddstr(win,y,x,str) \
    (wmove(win,y,x)==ERR?ERR:waddstr(win,str))
```

Now we can rewrite the above code to print "Hello World" like this:

```
mvwaddstr(win,10,5,"Hello World");
wrefresh(win);
```

The `<curses.h>` file contains many of these pseudo-functions to aid the creation of *curses* applications. Since these functions are macros, you will have to be careful how you structure your code. Certain features of the C language that normally apply to real functions are not possible with macro functions. For instance, you cannot reference the address of a macro. Be particularly careful with function arguments. In the following example, the call to `getyx()` is illegal and will cause the compiler to fail:

```
int y, x;
getyx(stdscr,&y,&x);    /* illegal */
```

The reason for this is quite simple: `getyx()` is not a function but a macro defined in `<curses.h>`. It is used to get the current `y,x` coordinates in a window. This is what it looks like:

```
#define getyx(win,y,x)    y = win->_cury, x = win->_curx
```

3.7 Other useful variables

Here is a list of other useful variables which may be defined in the <curses.h>
file on your system:

char ttytype[]   The function longname() uses this variable to extract the
                   name of the current terminal type. It is originally set up by
                   the function setupterm() which is automatically called by
                   initscr().

char *Def_term   This external variable is used to set up a default terminal
                   type if *curses* is unable to obtain it via the environment
                   variable **TERM**. By default, Def_term is set up for terminal
                   type "unknown". If you want to change the default setting
                   you must do this before calling initscr().

char *My_term   This variable is now obsolete; it was formerly used for
                   overriding any environment **TERM** setting. It was also used
                   instead of the variable Def_term.

chtype   chtype is not a variable; it is the base name of a storage
                   class (or type). *Curses* uses this storage class to store a
                   character along with attributes. It is normally typedefed to
                   an unsigned short or char. However, contrary to what is
                   said in the header file, this variable is not configurable and
                   cannot be changed, unless of course, you have a source code
                   license.

bool   Also a type rather than a variable, this is a synonym for
                   boolean although it is actually typedefed as a char.

char *acs_map   This is a pointer to the Alternate Character Set (ACS) as
                   defined in the terminfo description file. These characters
                   are used for line drawing. This is a new feature, made
                   available since the release of UNIX System V.3 (see Section
                   5.3).

If you are running a *termcap* version of *curses*, you will also have defined a set
of two-character variables representing the capabilities of the terminal. *Curses*
initializes these variables from the information obtained in the terminal
description, using the function setterm(). These two-character variables are
defined in the <curses.h> include file, but they are no longer supported under
UNIX System V.

3.8 Mini *curses*

Mini *curses* is a small version of *curses*; in fact it is really only a subset of the
full *curses* function library. It is, therefore, smaller and faster than the full *curses*
package, but mini *curses* does not allow you to work with more than one
window. In fact, the only window you can use is `stdscr`. Also, mini *curses* does
not support functions which can read from a window. Table 3.2 lists the functions
that are not part of the mini *curses* subset:

Table 3.2

FUNCTIONS NOT AVAILABLE USING MINICURSES			
`box()`	`clrtobot()`	`clrtoeol()`	`delch()`
`deleteln()`	`delwin()`	`getch()`	`getstr()`
`inch()`	`insch()`	`insertln()`	`longname()`
`mvdelch()`	`mvgetch()`	`mvgetstr()`	`mvinch()`
`mvinsch()`	`mvprintw()`	`mvscanw()`	`mvwaddch()`
`mvwaddstr()`	`mvwdelch()`	`mvwgetch()`	`mvwgetstr()`
`mvwin()`	`mvwinch()`	`mvwinsch()`	`mvwprintw()`
`mvwscanw()`	`newwin()`	`overlay()`	`overwrite()`
`printw()`	`putp()`	`scanw()`	`scroll()`
`setscrreg()`	`subwin()`	`touchwin()`	`vidattr()`
`waddch()`	`waddstr()`	`wclear()`	`wclrtobot()`
`wclrtoeol()`	`wdelch()`	`wdeleteln()`	`werase()`
`wgetch()`	`wgetstr()`	`winsch()`	`winsertln()`
`wmove()`	`wprintw()`	`wrefresh()`	`wscanw()`
`wsetscrreg()`			

Mini *curses* arrived with UNIX System V versions of *curses*, but has since been
dropped and was never documented. Although it seemed a good idea at the time,
it was discovered that the savings in mini *curses* was insignificant. You may still
find that it is implemented on your system, although it isn't supported any more.

The `<curses.h>` file contains macros for use with mini *curses*; some of
them are defined as deliberate non-existent functions, placed there so that an
error is generated at compile time, just in case you used a function which is not
part of the mini *curses* subset.

To compile a program using mini *curses*, use -**DMINICURSES** as an option
to **cc** on the command line.

cc -DMINICURSES -o file file.c -lcurses

3.9 Other definitions

The function `wgetch()` is used to get character input from a window. This function returns an `int`. If a function key is pressed and the keypad is enabled, `getch()` will return an integer representation of the function key depressed. You can test what function key was depressed by comparing the many constants defined in `<curses.h>` with the return value.

A list of alternate character set constants is also defined, but all these variables, including the function key constants, are only defined in the newer terminfo versions of *curses*.

CHAPTER 4

General program format

Our next step is to learn how to create a *curses* program. Before doing this, you need to understand the structure of a *curses*-based program, and this chapter takes you through these basics. It includes how to enter and leave a *curses* program, how to modify the terminal's operating modes, and how to get input from the keyboard and display it on the terminal screen.

4.1 Basic program structure

The basic structure of a *curses* program is as follows:

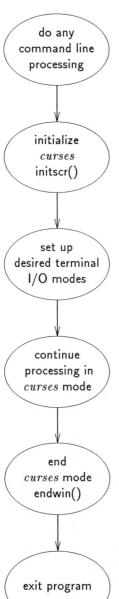

Before starting *curses* up, it is a good idea to do any command line processing first. For example, if the user did not enter a valid argument on the command line, your program would probably want to print a message to stderr using fprintf(3) and then exit the program. Do not enter into *curses* mode until you are ready to do so.

Many internal structures and variables must be set up before *curses* is ready for use. Therefore, *curses* must be initialized. This is normally done with initscr() which sets up the provided windows curscr and stdscr, initializes the terminal, and then places the program into an *in-curses* mode.

If you want to set any special I/O modes in the terminal driver, this should be done after initialization. These modes are normally set up once only, and then remain unmodified throughout program execution. For example, the terminal is put into *raw* mode, *echoing* is turned off, and so on.

The program now operating in *curses* mode can continue processing with the *curses* facilities. For example, create/delete windows, add characters to a window, get keyboard input, and so on.

When processing is complete and the program is ready to return to the shell (or calling process), the terminal must first be placed back into its original operating modes, the modes that were current before entering into the program. This is done with endwin().

Finally, exit the program.

Let us take a look at a simple *curses* program:

```
#include <curses.h>

main()
{
    initscr();
    move((LINES - 1)/2, (COLS - 1)/2);
    addstr("a very simple curses program");
    refresh();
    endwin();
    exit(0);
}
```

Several points about this little program are worth making. First of all, it assumes that the environment variable **$TERM** is set to reflect the terminal type. You do not have to physically test for this yourself as it is done automatically within initscr(). Secondly, because we have not used a function prefixed with w, we are not specifying a window. In fact, we are working with the provided window stdscr which is initialized by initscr() and defined in <curses.h>. We could have written the same program like this:

```
#include <curses.h>

main()
{
    initscr();
    wmove(stdscr,(LINES - 1)/2, (COLS - 1)/2);
    waddstr(stdscr,"a very simple curses program");
    wrefresh(stdscr);
    endwin();
}
```

This is roughly what the previous example program would look like after it had been through the C preprocessor. In Chapter 3 we learned that *curses* provides some convenient routines which are specifically set up for use with stdscr. In the first example we used those routines; in the second example we specify the window with which *curses* is to operate. This program does not do very much, but it does outline how a *curses* program should start and end.

The function initscr() is used to initialize *curses*. It allocates space for the two windows curscr and stdscr, sets up LINES, COLS and other external variables, and places the terminal into an *in-curses* mode. The function endwin() is used to place the program back into its original *out-of-curses* mode. In our example, we do not process any input, so we don't set any special terminal

I/O modes.

If we were to process input, we would probably want to turn echo off. To do this we would use the function `noecho()`. This would enable us to process input without displaying characters entered at the keyboard. This is useful for programs like the UNIX editor *vi* which need to process the input in case the key typed was a command key. For example, in *vi*, the **Escape** key places the editor into command mode.

Our example program uses the function `move()` to place the cursor in the middle of the terminal screen. Notice the parameters of this function: the first parameter is the `y` coordinate, and the second is the `x` coordinate. It also uses variables `LINES` and `COLS` defined in the `<curses.h>` file. These variables contain the dimensions of the terminal screen. By dividing each of these variables by 2, we can figure out how to find the center of the terminal screen, irrespective of the terminal type. Also, note how both `LINES` and `COLS` are decremented. This is because *curses* uses a 0 (zero)-based coordinate system (see Figure 1.1). If `LINES` equals 25, for example, then we can only address lines 0 to 24. Similarly, if `COLS` equals 80, we can only address columns 0 to 79.

The function `addstr()` is used to add a string to a window. In this case it is `stdscr`. The string is placed on the terminal screen at whichever y,x coordinates the window cursor is set to. In this case it would be the center of the screen, since we have just issued a call to move there.

At this point in the program, nothing has appeared on the physical screen simply because the program has been working with a virtual terminal screen `stdscr`, and not the real physical screen. To make the real terminal screen look like the virtual screen, we now use the function `refresh()`, which reflects any changes made to a window (in this case `stdscr`) to be updated on the real terminal screen.

Finally, `endwin()` is called, which generally does a clean-up to restore the terminal to how it was originally set up before *curses* was invoked. If this is not done, the program will remain in *curses* mode even after it has terminated. This often leaves the terminal driver in an undesirable state. Consequently, the user is left confused by the sudden change in the way the terminal behaves.

4.2 Setting terminal input modes

Under normal operation the terminal operates in *full-duplex* mode. In other words, when characters are typed at the keyboard, they are echoed back to the terminal via the computer. Characters may be typed at any time, even if output is still occurring. The *tty* device driver buffers input characters as they are received in a system character input buffer (*clist*). If the input buffer overflows (which is extremely rare), or if the total characters in the buffer exceed the system-specified limit without a process reading them, characters may be lost. In fact, when the input limit is reached, all currently buffered characters are discarded.

Normally, input is processed in units of lines which are delimited by a new-line (NL), end-of-line (EOL), or end-of-file (EOF) character. This means a process attempting to read from the terminal device is suspended until a delimiting character is received. However, certain characters received by the driver have special meaning, and the driver interprets them depending on how it is configured. They are as follows:

Interrupt	*(Rubout or ASCII DEL)* Generates an interrupt signal which is received by all running processes associated with the terminal. A process receiving this signal terminates, unless it has been programmed to ignore it.
Quit	*(Control-|)* Identical to **Interrupt**, except that a file is created in the current directory containing a *core* image of the process.
Stop	*(Control-S)* Temporarily suspends output to the terminal.
Start	*(Control-Q)* Resumes output currently suspended by **Stop**.
Erase	*(#)* Erases the last character typed, but will not erase beyond the start of a line, as delimited by a NL, EOL, or EOF character. This is often set to Control-H.
Kill	*(@)* Deletes the entire line, as delimited by a NL, EOF, or EOL character. This is often set to Control-C or Control-U.
New-Line	*(ASCII NL)* Line delimiter (satisfies the read). Characters stored in the *tty* driver's internal buffer are passed over to the process which is reading from the terminal and the buffer is flushed.

Curses retains these terminal modes by default. Consequently, this makes problems for programs which must know exactly what keys have been depressed, without being interpreted. Also, in most cases, an interactive *curses* program should not be kept waiting for a *new-line* character to be typed at the keyboard.

To combat these problems, *curses* provides a comprehensive set of routines for setting and reading the terminal driver modes. These functions are summarized as follows:

`cbreak()`	Sets the terminal into **cbreak** mode. This means that characters typed at the terminal are not buffered by the *tty* driver; they become

immediately available to the program as they are entered at the keyboard, without having to wait for a line delimiter. The *tty* driver continues to process interrupt, quit, start and stop characters, but canonical processing (erase and kill) is turned off. Pre-System V versions of *curses* used crmode() for this function which has now been replaced by cbreak().

nocbreak()

Resets the terminal out of **cbreak** mode. Characters entered at the keyboard are now buffered by the *tty* driver, and input is processed in units of lines. Once again, this function replaces the old nocrmode() function found on pre-System V versions of *curses*.

raw()

The terminal is set into *raw* mode. This works the same way cbreak() mode does, except that **all** characters are passed directly to the program without being interpreted. This includes interrupt, quit, start and stop characters. *Raw* mode also places the terminal into 8-bit transmission mode (see meta()).

noraw()

The terminal is set back into 7-bit transmission mode, and characters are buffered on input. This function undoes what was set up by raw().

echo()

Used in conjunction with wgetch(). If echo is enabled, then wgetch() automatically adds characters typed at the keyboard to the working window. When the window is refreshed the characters read by wgetch() are sent back to the terminal. wgetch() uses waddch() internally to add characters to a window. Other input functions may be used in a similar way, such as wgetstr() and wscanw().

Note that at all times echo() is turned off in the *tty* driver by *curses*. If keys are typed on the keyboard without being read, they will not be echoed on the screen. It is up to the programmer to read characters and choose the method by which *curses* handles them. In other words, even if echo() is called, characters will not be echoed back to the terminal unless the characters have been read and the window refreshed.

noecho()

In this mode, characters are not added to the window by wgetch(). It is up to you to add them to it. This is normally done with waddch() followed by wrefresh(). This mode is often required by programs which have to do their own echoing, possibly in a controlled area of the screen, or if the characters entered are control characters specific to the program, specifying some action. This type of character is often not displayed at all.

nodelay(win,bf)

If bf is TRUE, this function makes the input function getch() a non-blocking call — that is, if no input is ready when getch() is called, getch() will not wait for input but will return ERR instead.

halfdelay(tenths)

Introduced in System V.3, this function is a cross between cbreak() and nodelay(). Basically, it is the same as cbreak() mode, except that this function sets up a time out of *tenths* of a second for future getch() calls. If there is no input from the keyboard, getch() will wait on input for the amount of time specified before timing out and returning ERR.

intrflush(win,bf)

If bf is TRUE, this function flushes out any pending characters in the *tty* driver output queue if an interrupt key is depressed on the keyboard. Responses to interrupts become much quicker, and this is in fact enabled by default. However, *curses* is supposed to know what the terminal screen looks like. If output is interrupted, *curses* still has the notion that the screen was updated successfully, even if the screen update has not been completed due to the interrupt. So, this function could cause *curses* to have the wrong idea of what is really on the terminal screen. Some systems like early 4BSD do not support this facility within their *tty* driver.

keypad(win,bf)

If bf is TRUE, this function will enable the **keypad**. By default the keypad is disabled: this means the function getch() will not treat special keys (such as arrow or function keys) any differently from ordinary alphanumeric keys on the keyboard. These keys normally send a sequence containing more than one character. For example, on the Wyse 50, if function key labeled F1 is depressed, the terminal sends the character sequence "**^[@**" (escape character followed by the @ character). Since getch() is a function which returns an integer, the value returned cannot reflect the sequence of characters generated by a function key. However, if the keypad is enabled, getch() will return an integer representation of the character sequence received. Of course, this is provided the sequence is defined in the terminal's terminfo description. These values returned are defined in <curses.h>. Note that on most modern terminals, function keys are programmable. This may cause problems to your program at run time if they have been programmed with different character sequences to those defined in the terminal's terminfo description.

meta(win,bf)

If bf is TRUE, getch() will return characters with all 8 bits, instead of the default 7 bits. Some systems cannot do 8-bit processing. This is a deficiency of the device driver, not *curses*. If it is not supported, ERR is returned.

notimeout(win,bf)

Introduced with System V.3, this function tells getch() not to timeout while waiting for the next input character. This may sound confusing, but on System V.3 the getch() function sets a timer while waiting for input if interpreting an escape sequence. This way, getch() can determine whether the escape sequence is the result of a function key being typed, or the user physically entering some escape sequence at the keyboard.

savetty()

This function saves the settings of the current terminal (*tty*) modes in an internal buffer. It is automatically called by initscr().

resetty()

This function restores the terminal (*tty*) modes to what was originally saved in the internal buffer, set by savetty().

baudrate()

This function returns an integer value representing the current **baud** rate. This is the current *bits per second* transmission rate setting within the *tty* driver (Note: not the setting of the terminal —

although it should obviously be the same). If 0 is returned the terminal is *off-line*. This may mean that the terminal is switched off or the communication path between the computer and the terminal has broken. If the terminal ought to be on-line, it might be worth issuing a `resetty()` call to try to bring the terminal *on-line*.

`erasechar()`

Returns the current *erase* character set in the *tty* driver.

`killchar()`

Returns the current *line-kill* character set in the *tty* driver.

`typeahead(fildes)`

Some users, especially data entry personnel, type characters at the keyboard so fast that the program cannot keep up. For this reason the function `typeahead()` is used periodically to check the terminal input buffer; if input is found, the current update is postponed until a `refresh()` call. This enables *curses* to respond to keys typed in advance. The file descriptor `fildes` specifies what device to check input on; this is normally 0 (`stdin`). If `fildes` is −1 then typeahead is turned off. A call to typeahead affects only the current screen (`curscr`).

`flushinp()`

If any input is pending in the *tty* driver input buffer, it is flushed out, and any typeahead is lost.

`reset_shell_mode()`

Available since System V, this routine restores the *tty* driver to the mode it was in before entering the *curses* program. It replaces the earlier version of the *curses* function `resetterm()`.

`reset_prog_mode()`

Available since System V, this resets the *tty* driver back into an *in-curses* mode. It replaces the earlier version of *curses* function `fixterm()`.

`draino(ms)`

When this function is called the program is suspended until the output character buffer queue has drained enough to complete in `ms` additional milliseconds. This function is not available on all systems. It is often provided, for compatibility reasons only, on systems that cannot provide this functionality. ERR is returned in such cases.

napms(ms)   This routine suspends the program for ms milliseconds, and works much the same way as the standard C-library function sleep(). However, this function can sleep for milliseconds, providing a higher resolution than the standard sleep function which can only handle seconds. It is especially efficient if the fast timer driver (available in the public domain) is installed in the kernel, but don't go searching for it unless you have a UNIX source license, because you will have to recompile *curses* to get it to work. Once again, this function is supported on some systems only.

nl(), nonl()   Both of these functions control the translation of a **new-line**. The default mode is nl() which translates a new-line into **carriage-return** and **linefeed** on output, and **return** is translated to **new-line** on input. The function nonl() disables this translation.

The terminal's operating modes are typically configured soon after calling initscr(). The following program demonstrates this.

```
#include <curses.h>
#include <ctype.h>

main()
{
    int c;
    int y,x;

    initscr();              /* initialize curses */
    noecho();               /* handle our own echo */
    keypad(stdscr,TRUE);    /* we use the arrow keys */
    typeahead(FALSE);       /* turn typeahead off */
    scrollok(stdscr,TRUE);  /* turn scroll on */

    /* HOME key on keypad finishes program */
    while((c = getch()) != KEY_HOME) {
        flushinp();
        getyx(stdscr,y,x);
        switch(c) {
            case KEY_UP:
                if(y - 1 >= 0)
```

```
                        move(--y,x);
                break;
            case KEY_DOWN:
                if(y < LINES -1)
                    move(++y,x);
                break;
            case KEY_LEFT:
                if(x - 1 >= 0)
                    move(y,--x);
                break;
            case KEY_RIGHT:
                if(x < COLS -1)
                    move(y,++x);
                break;
            default:
                if(isalnum(c) || isspace(c))
                    addch(c);
                else
                    beep();
        }
        refresh();
    }
    endwin();
}
```

After initializing *curses* and setting up for the run, this program goes into a loop, reading characters until the user presses the key marked "home" on the keypad. Each key input is tested. If an arrow key is pressed the cursor moves in the desired direction. Otherwise, if getch() returns a printable character, it is added to stdscr using addch().

Note the call to flushinp(). When keypad() is enabled, *curses* pays special attention to escape sequences sent by function, arrow and other special keys on the keyboard. When one of these keys is depressed it sends a sequence of characters which is interpreted by getch(). If getch() recognizes the sequence, it returns an integer value representing the key which was depressed. These values are defined in the <curses.h> file. If the key depressed has not been defined within the terminal's terminfo description, each character in the character sequence generated by the arrow keys, is returned on subsequent calls to getch(). This may have an undesirable effect if the unwanted characters returned are processed by the program. The call to flushinp() fixes this by telling *curses* to flush the input queue so that getch() is now waiting on an empty buffer.

4.3 Creating windows

If we want to use a window other than the default windows supplied by *curses* (stdscr and curscr), we need to create it before we can access it. *Curses* provides the function newwin(lines,cols,begy,begx) for this purpose. The newwin() function requires 4 arguments. These arguments tell *curses* the dimensions of your new window, and where you want the new window placed on the terminal screen.

The arguments are specified as follows:

lines   The maximum *vertical* dimension of the new window, specified in units of lines.

cols   The maximum *horizontal* dimension of the new window, specified in units of columns.

begy   The *line* coordinate, specifying where the new window will start in relation to the stdscr vertical dimension.

begx   The *column* coordinate, specifying where the new window will start in relation to the stdscr horizontal dimension.

newwin() computes the dimensions of the new window by using the following equations:

```
if(begy + lines > LINES)
    lines = LINES - begy;

if(begx + cols > COLS)
    cols = COLS - begx;

if(lines == 0)
    lines = LINES - begy;

if(cols == 0)
    cols = COLS - begx;
```

Therefore, if the arguments to newwin() are newwin(0,0,0,0), this is the same, in effect, as newwin(LINES,COLS,0,0), and the size of the new window will be the size of the terminal screen.

The dimensions of the new window must be equal to or within the maximum dimensions of the stdscr window, which is specified in the variables LINES and COLS.

The following example creates a window which is 10 lines high by 40 columns across, and it is placed in relation to `stdscr` at line 5, column 10:

```
#include <curses.h>

main()
{
    WINDOW *new;

    initscr();
    noecho();
    nodelay(stdscr,TRUE);

    if(LINES < 10 || COLS < 40)
        fatal_err("terminal screen too small");

    new = newwin(10,40,5,10);
    if(new == (WINDOW *)NULL)
        fatal_err("memory error");

    /* processing continues */
}


fatal_err(str)
char *str;
{
    mvprintw(LINES - 1, 0, "Fatal Error: %s\n",str);
    refresh();
    endwin();
    exit(1);
}
```

This is a typical way to start a *curses* program. After initializing *curses* with `initscr()`, the terminal operating modes are set. `newwin()` is then called to initialize a new `WINDOW` structure. However, if `newwin()` cannot allocate enough memory for it, it will fail and `(WINDOW *)NULL` is returned. The program then calls `fatal_err()`, which prints the error message to the lower left-hand side of the terminal screen. This routine `mvprintw()` is used for this.

Routines prefixed with `mv` are normally macros defined in `<curses.h>`, but since `mvprintw()` uses variable arguments similar to `printf()`, it has been implemented as a real function. The `mv` prefix indicates that a move is to be done before the string is printed. The extra arguments specify the new location. We could have written it like this:

```
move(LINES - 1, 0);
printw("Fatal Error: %s\n",str);
```

The function `printw()` does exactly the same as `mvprintw()`, but without the move. Note that both of these functions operate on `stdscr`. If we wanted to use a specific window we could have used `wprintw()`. The following examples demonstrate this:

```
wprintw(stdscr,"Fatal Error: %s\n",str);
```

This is the same as:

```
printw("Fatal Error: %s\n",str);
```

Similarly, to do the move at the same time we could say:

```
mvwprintw(stdscr, LINES - 1, 0, "Fatal Error: %s\n",str);
```

This is the same as:

```
mvprintw(LINES - 1, 0, "Fatal Error: %s\n",str);
```

Note that even though the `mv` prefix is before the `w` the window is always specified first.

The following program provides a limited windowing environment for ASCII-based terminals. It uses `newwin()` to create two windows in which a shell is spawned. To switch between windows you use the escape character, and Control-D ends the program. It also uses some advanced UNIX programming techniques which are not within the scope of this book. It is an interesting little program, not complete, but one you may wish to build upon.

```
/*
 * Program: wsh
 *
 * Description: a two window multiplexing
 *              interactive shell
 *
 */

#include <curses.h>
#include <signal.h>
#include <fcntl.h>
```

```
/*
 * max number of multiplexed windows
 */
#define MAX_WIN      2

#define MAXBUF       128

/*
 * template of a mux channel
 */
typedef struct {
    WINDOW *win;    /* curses win for this channel */
    int out[2];     /* pipe output descriptors */
    int err[2];     /* pipe error descriptors */
    int in[2];      /* pipe input descriptors */
    int pid;        /* pid of process */
} WIN;

WIN w[MAX_WIN];    /* the mux array */

/*
 * template of window positions
 */
typedef struct {
    int lines; /* how many lines in win */
    int cols;  /* how many columns in win */
    int begy;  /* what line to start from */
    int begx;  /* what column to start from */
} WINPOS;

static WINPOS pos[MAX_WIN] = {
    /*
     * (N.B)
     * Assumes that the terminals dimensions
     * are 24 x 80
     */
    { 11, 79, 0, 0 }, /* spec of 1st win */
    { 10, 79, 14, 0 },/* spec of 2nd win */
};

/*
 */
#define lns(x)       pos[x].lines
#define cls(x)       pos[x].cols
```

```
#define bgy(x)        pos[x].begy
#define bgx(x)        pos[x].begx


main()
{
    char buf[MAXBUF];
    register x;
    int n,c;
    int child();
    int cwin = 0; /* current window */

    signal(SIGCLD,child);

    create_windows();
    create_shells();

    nodelay(stdscr,TRUE);
    noecho();
    raw();

    winbar(" Top Window");

    for(x = MAX_WIN - 1; x >= 0; x--)
        wrefresh(w[x].win);


    /*
     * we have to poll on each pipe
     * input descriptor and also keyboard input,
     * This would be better implemented using
     * streams (i.e poll()).
     */
    while(1) {

        /*
         * read from each channel non blocking
         * if anything is there then display its data
         */
        for(x = 0; x < MAX_WIN; x++) {

            /*
             * stdout channel
             */
```

```
        if((n = read(w[x].in[0],buf,MAXBUF - 1)) > 0) {
            buf[n] = '\0';
            waddstr(w[x].win,buf);
        }

        /*
         * stderr channel
         *
         * we only read this if nothing is coming
         * in from stdout channel because we need
         * to synchronize the input.
         *
         * if we don't do this then we may get
         * stderr stuff merged in with stdout stuff.
         */
        if(n == 0) {
            if((n=read(w[x].err[0],buf,MAXBUF - 1)) > 0){
                buf[n] = '\0';
                waddstr(w[x].win,buf);
            }
        }

        /*
         * if we read something, update screen
         */
        if(n > 0)
            wnoutrefresh(w[x].win);
    }

    /*
     * Read from the keyboard and add to
     * current win, also push any input down
     * the pipe output descriptor to whatever
     * shell is currently waiting at the
     * other end of the pipe.
     */
    x = 0;
    while((c = getch()) > 0) {
        switch(c) {

        /*
         * ESCAPE key means switch window
         */
        case 0x1b:
```

```
            if(cwin == MAX_WIN - 1) {
                cwin = 0;
                winbar(" Top Window");
            }
            else {
                cwin++;
                winbar(" Bottom Window");
            }
            break;

        /*
         * end program
         */
        case 4 : /* Ctrl D */
            fatal("");

        /*
         * add the character to our screen
         * buffer and poke it down the pipe
         * to the receiving shell
         */
        default:
            buf[x++] = c;
            write(w[cwin].out[1],&c,1);
        }
    }

    /*
     * got some chars so display them
     */
    if(x) {
        buf[x] = '\0';
        waddstr(w[cwin].win,buf);
    }

    /*
     * finally, update our screen
     */
    wnoutrefresh(w[cwin].win);
    doupdate();
    }
}

/*
```

```
 * draw a line between windows
 */
winbar(s)
char *s;
{
    standout();
    mvprintw(12,0,"%-79s",s);
    standend();
    refresh();
}



create_windows()
{
    register x;
    WINDOW *getnewwin();

    initscr();
    for(x = 0; x < MAX_WIN; x++) {
        if(getnewwin(&w[x],x) == (WINDOW *)NULL)
            fatal("window creation error");
        scrollok(w[x].win,TRUE);
    }
}

fatal(s)
char *s;
{
    clear();
    refresh();
    mvcur(0,0,LINES - 1,0);
    /*
     * fix the bug in system V.2
     */
    nodelay(stdscr,FALSE);
    endwin();
    printf("%s\n",s);
    exit(1);
}


/*
 * creates the new windows
 * in which we spawn the shells into
```

```
 */
WINDOW *getnewwin(m,x)
WIN *m;
int x;
{
    return(m->win = newwin(lns(x),cls(x),bgy(x),bgx(x)));
}


create_shells()
{
    register x;

    for(x = 0; x < MAX_WIN; x++)
        make_sh(w[x].out,w[x].in,w[x].err,&w[x].pid);
}


make_sh(out,in,err,pid)
int out[];
int in[];
int err[];
int *pid;
{
    int ctl;

    if(pipe(out) < 0 || pipe(in) < 0 || pipe(err) < 0)
        fatal("pipe failure");

    switch(*pid = fork()) {
    case -1:
        fatal("fork failed");

    case 0:
        /*
         * CHILD PROCESS
         *
         * We are the child here, we have
         * to arrange our file descriptors
         * so that we no longer write to the
         * tty driver direct. all descriptors
         * 0,1 & 2 are now fathomed through our
         * software pipes back to the parent.
         *
```

```
     */
    if(close(0) < 0)
        fatal("close failed stdin");
    if(dup(out[0]) != 0)
        fatal("dup failed stdin");
    if(close(1) < 0)
        fatal("close failed stdout");
    if(dup(in[1]) != 1)
        fatal("dup failed stdout");
    if(close(2) < 0)
        fatal("close failed stderr");
    if(dup(err[1]) != 2)
        fatal("dup failed stderr");

    if(
        close(out[0]) < 0
        ||
        close(out[1]) < 0
        ||
        close(in[0]) < 0
        ||
        close(in[1]) < 0
        ||
        close(err[0]) < 0
        ||
        close(err[1]) < 0
    )
        fatal("close failed in child");

    /*
     * start the shell
     */
    execlp("sh","sh","-i",0);
    fatal("exec failure");
}

/*
 * PARENT PROCESS CONTINUES
 */
if(
    close(out[0]) < 0
    ||
    close(in[1]) < 0
    ||
```

```
            close(err[1]) < 0
    )
        fatal("parent close failure");

    /*
     * now set the input descriptors for NO DELAY
     * so that we don't have to hang awaiting input
     * on it.
     */
    if((ctl = fcntl(in[0],F_GETFL,0)) < 0)
        fatal("fcntl failed get on input");

    if(fcntl(in[0],F_SETFL,ctl | O_NDELAY) < 0)
        fatal("fcntl failed set on input");

    if((ctl = fcntl(err[0],F_GETFL,0)) < 0)
        fatal("fcntl failed get on err");

    if(fcntl(err[0],F_SETFL,ctl | O_NDELAY) < 0)
        fatal("fcntl failed set on err");

    /*
     * Thats it, all set up for i/o through
     * the software pipe.
     *
     * Input from this pipe now setup in in[0]
     * Output for this pipe now setup in out[1]
     * Err to this pipe now setup in err[0]
     *
     */
}


child()
{
    fatal("Child died");
}
```

Basically, two windows are created in the function create_windows(). Inside this function we set up the windows so that scrolling is allowed in each (scrollok()). The two shells are then created by create_shells(). All file descriptors are reassigned so that the parent process handles I/O through software pipes. The function nodelay(stdscr,TRUE) sets up stdscr so that it will not block and hang the program if no input is waiting on an input pipe. After some initialization the program enters a loop which is terminated by typing

Control-D, in which case endwin() is called to clean up.

Each channel is tested for input; if there is any, it is added to the current window with waddstr(), then wnoutrefresh() is called to update the current virtual window. After checking the keyboard input with getch(), received characters are pushed down the relevant pipe to the receiving shell and are then added to the current window: doupdate() is called to cause the physical screen update.

The program creates the effect of two independent windows on the terminal screen with a shell running in each. Most programs will run in these windows except, oddly enough, *curses* programs.

As an exercise, try to get *vi* working in one of the windows.

4.4 Adding characters to a window

The most primitive way to add a character to a window is by using waddch(win,ch). This function is used by all *curses* functions which add characters to a window in some way. We could say that waddch() is the lowest level *curses* function used to add a character to a window.

On later versions of *curses*, waddch() uses a character of type chtype defined in <curses.h>. It is important that you use this type whenever you work with *curses* functions to keep your program compatible with future versions of the library.

All characters are added with *attributes* if set. If, for example, the *standout* attribute is turned on, the character is added to the window in *standout* mode. Also, depending on what input modes are set, waddch() may translate certain characters. If the character is a control character, the character is added to the window in a printable form. That is, Control-G will look like '**^G**' on the screen. If the character is a **TAB**, it will be expanded into blanks on the screen. If it is a **new-line** and new-line mapping is turned on (nl()), the line is cleared from the current cursor position to the end of the line, and the cursor is placed at the beginning of the next line.

There are numerous *high-level* functions which provide similar services. For example, the function waddstr(win,str) is used to add a NULL terminated string to a window. waddstr() scans along the string until the terminating NULL character is reached, adding each individual character to the window with waddch().

In keeping with the philosophy of UNIX, that is, **Build on the work of others**, the standard I/O package function printf() has been implemented in the *curses* package as wprintw(). This function actually uses the standard printf() function to expand the format string argument. It then adds it to the given window with waddstr(). This means that you can format a string and pass it to wprintw() as an argument, just as you would with printf().

4.5 Moving around a window

To move to a new position within a window you use the `wmove(win,y,x)` function. The new coordinates must be within the bounds of the window's maximum dimensions or `ERR` is returned and the coordinates are not changed. The function sets the `_cury` and `_curx` positions to the y,x parameters passed. However, although its instructions are immediate, it requires a `wrefresh()` call to take effect.

This function is rarely used on its own. Usually you would want to move to a particular location within a window and print a message of some sort, or read something from the keyboard and display characters typed at some location other than where the cursor is. For this reason, a set of *move macros* are provided in the `<curses.h>` header file.

To move to a new location and then add a character you could, for example, use `mvwaddch(win,y,x,ch)`. The parameters for *mv-macros* and *mv-functions* are consistent. That is, they all require a new y,x location. This example uses `mvwaddstr()`:

```
#include <curses.h>

main()
{
    WINDOW *mywin;

    initscr();
    mywin = newwin(10,40,5,10);
    if(mywin == (WINDOW *)NULL) {
        mvaddstr(LINES - 1,0,"memory error");
        refresh();
        endwin();
        exit(1);
    }

    mvwaddstr(mywin,10/2,40/2,"Hello World");
    wrefresh(mywin);
    endwin();
    exit(0);
}
```

A function prefixed with `mv` uses the `move()` function, and requires at least two arguments: the new y,x coordinates to move to. Some routines are prefixed with both `mv` and `w`, and in this case the `mv` prefix is placed before the `w` prefix, but the window argument is always specified first. For example, the functions `mvprintw()` and `mvwprintw()` are effectively the same, in that both functions print a string to a window at a specified location. The only exception is that mvprintw() is not window-specific. It is used solely to print to stdscr, and so does not require a window argument.

Notice that the error message uses mvaddstr() while the function that prints the string uses mvwaddstr(). The error message is printed to stdscr. The string "Hello World" is printed in the window mywin which we create using newwin(). Note also that refresh() is used for stdscr and wrefresh() is used for mywin.

Sometimes a temporary move to a new location is necessary. For example, you may want to print an error message at the bottom of the screen and return the cursor to where it was before the move took place. Although *curses*, unfortunately, does not provide a function for this, it can be done.

The following set of routines is provided as a supplement to the *curses* library package. These functions enable you to *temporarily* move to a specified location on a window and print some text there. They will only work on System V versions of UNIX, and only if your system supports varargs (see Section 5 of the UNIX Programmer's Manual).

Note: if you intend to port a *curses* program using these routines to another UNIX machine, you must also port these routines. It is probably a good idea to create a separate library for them, which you can port along with your programs.

Keeping in line with the rest of the *curses* package we use macros for the stdscr-specific routines. You will need to create another include file for these. I have called it <excurses.h>:

```
#define addstryx(y,x,str) wprintwyx(stdscr,y,x,str)
#define addchyx(y,x,ch) waddchyx(stdscr,y,x,ch)
#define waddstryx(win,y,x,str) wprintwyx(win,y,x,str)



#include <curses.h>
#include <varargs.h>

waddchyx(win,y,x,ch)
WINDOW *win;
int y,x;
chtype ch;
{
     register yy,xx;
     int ret;

     getyx(win,yy,xx);
     if(wmove(win,y,x) == ERR)
          return(ERR);
```

```
        ret = waddch(win,ch);
        (void)wmove(win,yy,xx);
        return(ret);
}




/* VARARGS */
printwyx(y,x,fmt,va_alist)
int y,x;
char *fmt;
va_dcl
{
        char buf[BUFSIZ];
        register yy,xx;
        int ret;
        va_list argp;

        getyx(stdscr,yy,xx);
        va_start(argp);

        if(move(y,x) == ERR)
            return(ERR);

        (void)vsprintf(buf,fmt,argp);
        ret = addstr(buf);
        (void)move(yy,xx);
        return(ret);
}


/* VARARGS */
wprintwyx(win,y,x,fmt,va_alist)
WINDOW *win;
int y,x;
char *fmt;
va_dcl
{
        char buf[BUFSIZ];
        register yy,xx;
        int ret;
        va_list argp;

        getyx(win,yy,xx);
```

```
        va_start(argp);

        if(wmove(win,y,x) == ERR)
            return(ERR);

        (void)vsprintf(buf,fmt,argp);
        ret = waddstr(win,buf);
        (void)wmove(win,yy,xx);
        return(ret);
}
```

The macro getyx(win,y,x) assigns the current y,x coordinates of the specified window to the two variables y and x supplied as parameters. If we retain these coordinates with getyx() before we move to a new location, we can return to them later. Note that getyx() is a macro defined in <curses.h>; you must not pass the addresses of y and x to it (see Section 3.6 for a definition of getyx()).

I have placed these functions into a file named **printyx.c**. They are compiled into object form, and placed into a library. On my system it is called **libexcurses.a**. Use the UNIX archive program **ar** with the following command:

ar qv libexcurses.a printyx.o

The following example program uses these functions. It starts by printing a string at the top of the screen, then temporarily moves to line 10 and prints another. Finally, the program continues to print a string from where it left off before any move took place. If you run this program, your screen should look something like that shown in Figure 4.1.

```
#include <curses.h>
#include <excurses.h>

main()
{
        initscr();
        addstr("Start text here --- ");
        printwyx(10,0,"This is line %d",10);
        addstryx(20,0,"This is at line 20");
        addstr("continuation of text");
        refresh();
        endwin();
}
```

```
Start text here --- continuation of text




This is line 10




This is at line 20
```

Figure 4.1

4.6 Reading from the keyboard

The function `wgetch(win)` is used to get keyboard input from a specified window (for `stdscr`, the `getch()` macro is used). Depending on what input modes are set, `wgetch()` returns the key typed at the keyboard. If echoing is turned on, `wgetch()` uses `waddch()` to add the character to the window. If the *keypad* is enabled for the specified window and a function key is depressed, `wgetch()` will return an appropriate value representing it. These values are defined in `<curses.h>` and are prefixed with `KEY_`. The following extract of code is typically used to test the return value from `wgetch()`. Note that the code assumes that the window `mywin` has already been created:

```
switch(getch()) {
    case KEY_F(1):
        waddstr(mywin,"Function Key 1 was pressed");
        break;
    case KEY_F(2):
        waddstr(mywin,"Function Key 2 was pressed");
        break;
    case KEY_HOME:
        waddstr(mywin,"Key marked \"home\" was pressed");
        break;
    case KEY_LEFT:
```

```
        waddstr(mywin,"Left arrow key was pressed");
        break;
    case KEY_NPAGE: /* next page key */
        waddstr(mywin,"Key marked \"Pgdn\" was pressed");
        break;
    case KEY_PPAGE: /* previous page key */
        waddstr(mywin,"Key marked \"Pgup\" was pressed");
        break;
    case '0': case '1': case '2': case '3': case '4':
    case '5': case '6': case '7': case '8': case '9':
        waddstr(mywin,"Numeric key was pressed");
        break;
    default:
        beep();
}
```

If `wgetch()` is to retain control of the terminal, either `noecho()`, `cbreak()` or `raw()` must be set. If one of these is not set, then `wgetch()` will set `cbreak()` for you. In this case, when `wgetch()` is finished, it will restore input modes to what they were originally set to before `wgetch()` was called.

If `nodelay` is set and there are no characters waiting in the input queue, `wgetch()` will return ERR. This is a useful feature; it saves the program hanging the terminal if no characters are typed.

Most interactive programs have to monitor the keyboard activity in some way, and the most common way of doing this is to use `cbreak()` and `noecho()`. This will allow you to process the input first before displaying it — maybe validate it, for example. Since characters are not echoed to the screen as they are read, you can use `waddch()` to add the character to a location of choice within a window of choice — maybe even discard it.

One extra bit of advice: don't use both the `cbreak()` and `raw()` function calls together; choose one only. Since both these functions set the *tty* driver input control modes, using both of them could have an undesirable effect.

There is an inherent bug in some System V.2 versions of *curses* using `nodelay()`. For some reason, if *nodelay* is set and not reset before exiting the program, an EOF is returned to the parent process that spawned the program. If this happens to be a login shell, the user running the program is logged off the system. This has been fixed in System V.3.

`wgetstr(win,str)` is also an input function. It reads a string into a window at the current y,x coordinates. It uses `getch()` internally to read characters into the window until a new-line character is received. The input string is also stored in the character buffer `str`, which is assumed to be big enough to hold it. Before reading input, `getstr()` calls `refresh()` on the window so that input is taken relative to the most current y,x coordinates of the window.

Another form of reading input into a window is to use
`wscanw(win,fmt,pointer ...)`, or `scanw(fmt,pointer ...)` for `stdscr`.
Both these functions perform a `scanf(3)` on a window, and actually use the
low-level parts of scanf, so the normal scanf rules apply.   `scanf()` is part of the
UNIX stdio package (see the UNIX Programmer's Manual for a more detailed
explanation of the `scanf()` function).

Within `wscanw()`, it uses `wgetstr()` to read in the string until a new-line
character is received. Characters are added to the window with `waddch()` unless
`noecho()` has been called. The following program asks the user to enter a value
between 0 and 255, then prints the value received in hexadecimal:

```
#include <curses.h>

#define MAXHEXVAL 255

main()
{
    int value;

    initscr();

    do {
        erase();
        mvprintw(LINES - 1, 0,"Enter value up to %d: ",
                  MAXHEXVAL);
        refresh();
        scanw("%d",&value);
    } while(value < 0 || value > MAXHEXVAL);

    mvprintw(10,10,"Value is %x Hex",value);
    refresh();
    getch();
    endwin();
}
```

4.7 Reading from a window

The only method of reading a character from a window is to use the pseudo-
function `winch(win)` (`inch()` for `stdscr`). This function returns the character
under the cursor at the current y,x coordinates of a window, although this
character may contain attributes if they are set, as well as the character itself.
The attributes can be masked out as follows:

```
    char c;
```

```
c = winch(win) & ~A_ATTRIBUTES;
```

You can also use `winch()` to alter the character at the current y,x coordinates. Let us say that we want to change the character at this location to the character 'A'. First of all we have to retrieve the attributes on their own so we can *OR* them back into the new character. If this is not done, the character is added without them:

```
chtype attrs;

attrs = winch(win) & ~A_CHARTEXT;
winch(win) = ('A' | attrs);
```

The constants `A_ATTRIBUTES` and `A_CHARTEXT` are defined along with other attribute constants in the `<curses.h>` header file. Notice that `attrs` is a chtype. The constant `A_ATTRIBUTES` is the mask for the attributes part of chtype, while `A_CHARTEXT` is the mask for the character part of it.

The main thing to remember here is that all the characters in a window are stored in the two-dimensional array `_y[][]` which is part of the window structure referring to the window you are working with; it's a bit like having a private memory map of the terminal screen (or at least a portion of it if not stdscr). These characters are stored with attributes if they are set. As an example, here is a function which implements a print screen. It reads the `_y[][]` array and writes output via `popen()`, which creates a software pipe between the process and the UNIX print spooler **lp**. If you want to print the whole screen you simply call `wprtscr(curscr)`:

```
wprtscr(win)
WINDOW *win;
{
    FILE *pfd;
    register int y,x;
    char c;

    if((pfd = popen("lp 2>&1 >/dev/null","w")) == (FILE *)NULL)
        return(-1);

    for(y = 0; y < win->_maxy; y++) {
        for(x = 0; x < win->_maxx; x++) {
            c = win->_y[y][x] &~ A_ATTRIBUTES;
            fputc(c,pfd);
        }
        fputc('\n',pfd);
    }
```

```
    pclose(pfd);
    return(0);
}
```

Here is a useful function that implements a gets() on a specified window. Its purpose is to read a string from the current y,x coordinates in a window up to its maximum width. wgets() places its information into the passed character buffer str which is assumed to be large enough to hold the information retrieved:

```
wgets(win,str)
WINDOW *win;
char *str;
{
    register int y,x;

    getyx(win,y,x);
    while(win->_curx < win->_maxx) {
        *str++ = winch(win) & ~A_ATTRIBUTES;
        win->_curx++;
    }
    *str = '\0';
    wmove(win,y,x);
}
```

4.8 Deleting characters in a window

The function wdelch(win) is used to delete a character under the cursor on the specified window. Each character along the current line after the cursor in the window is shifted left one position and the last character becomes blank. The current y,x coordinates remain unchanged.

Other functions provided for deleting characters are fairly self-explanatory. The function wclrtobot(win) clears the window to spaces from the current y,x coordinates to the bottom of the window. wclrtoeol(win) clears the current line to spaces from the current y,x coordinate to the right-most edge of the specified window (note that neither of these functions have associated move macros). The function deleteln(win) is used to delete the current line; each line below the current line is shifted up one and the bottom line is rendered blank. Once again the current y,x coordinates remain unchanged.

The function wclear(win) clears the whole window to blanks from start to finish. The current y,x coordinates are reset to the *home* position, that is, y = 0, x = 0. If the specified window is a full window, that is, its size is equal to the dimensions of the terminal screen as outlined in the terminfo entry, clear() sets the _clear flag to TRUE, which sends the escape sequence for a clear-screen to the terminal the next time the window is refreshed. `werase(win)` performs the same function as `wclear()` except that a clear-screen sequence is not generated when refresh is called. (Note that neither of these functions have associated move macros.)

4.9 Inserting

The two functions associated with inserting into a window are `winsch(win,ch)` and `winsertln(win)`. The function `winsch()` is used to insert the character `ch` into the window `win` at the current y,x coordinates. The character at the current y,x coordinates and each character after it on the current line is shifted right by one and the last character on the line is lost. The function `winsertln()` inserts a line above the current one. The current line and each line below it on the window is shifted down by one, with the last line disappearing. The current y,x coordinates remain unchanged. This means the new y,x coordinates are now placed on the new blank line inserted, but not necessarily at the beginning of that line. Both these functions may cause the window to scroll if the `_scroll` flag was set on the window with `scrollok()`.

4.10 Overlaying windows

The two functions associated with overlaying windows are `overlay(win1,win2)` and `overwrite(win1,win2)`. A few points need to be cleared first before we discuss how these functions work.

The process of overlaying windows causes the contents of the overlapping portion of what is in one window (say win1) to be copied to the other window (say win2). This is only ever true if win1's coordinates happen to overlap win2's coordinates. The copy is always permanent; that is, characters that existed in win2 and were overwritten by win1 are lost.

Incidentally, this process is different to overlapping windows. For example, if you move a window to a new location and it happens to overlap another window, the window simply hides the overlapping portion of the window below it. There is no physical moving of any characters between the two windows and the data within each window remains unchanged.

The functions `overlay()` and `overwrite()` both copy permanently the overlapping portion of win1 into win2. Note that `overlay()` does this *non-destructively*; that is, blank characters are not copied, and characters in win2 which would be rendered blank remain unchanged. However, all other characters within the overlapping portion of the window are copied to win2. The function `overwrite()` is exactly the same as `overlay()`, but is *destructive*: that is, all characters including blanks are copied.

4.11 Windows within windows

The function subwin(win,lines,cols,begy,begx) creates a new window and returns a pointer to it. However, this window has a physical association with the parent window as specified in the parameter win. The new window's dimensions are set with the parameters lines and cols, and the starting location of the window within the parent are specified by the parameters begy and begx. These parameters are specified in relation to the overall terminal dimensions such as that defined in stdscr; they are not related to the parent windows HOME position 0,0.

Either or both of the parameters lines and cols may be 0. subwin() computes the new windows dimensions as follows:

```
if(lines == 0)
    lines = ((win->_maxy - win->_begy) - begy);
if(cols == 0)
    cols = ((win->_maxx - win_begx) - begx);
```

The new sub-window must fit within the bounds of the parent window, otherwise (WINDOW *)NULL is returned.

The new window is created within the parent window, and changes to either of them within the area overlapped by the sub-window will be made to both windows. Because the new sub-window is of a type WINDOW, it can be manipulated using any *curses* function which uses a window as an argument.

4.12 Deleting a window

The process of deleting a window loses the contents of it and all space associated with it is freed up. The function which does this is delwin(win). If the window has any associated sub-windows they should be deleted first, because delwin() does not delete sub-windows automatically, although by deleting the parent window it effectively invalidates the sub-window. It is important to do this so that memory is freed up for other uses. Also, if you access a sub-window after the parent is deleted, your program may dump core which will almost definitely leave the terminal in an unpredictable state.

4.13 Relocating a window

The function mvwin(win,begy,begx) is used to relocate a window. The given window is moved to the new location as specified by begy and begx, whose coordinates are the window's new top left-hand corner coordinates. The move must not allow the window or portion of it to overlap the terminal screen; if it does, the window is not moved and the function returns ERR.

When a window is moved from one location to another, the internal WINDOW data structure remains intact except, of course, _begy and _begx. This means that characters displayed with attributes will retain them throughout the move.

4.14 Forcing an update

Curses maintains full optimization at all times. Sometimes it is necessary to force *curses* to throw away any optimization about what parts of a window it has already updated on the terminal screen. For example, the following function provides a shell escape from within a *curses* program. The function starts by saving the context of the *curses* environment by using savetty(), which saves the current settings of the terminal driver in an internal buffer. The function reset_shell_mode() is then called, which places the terminal into the modes it was originally set into before entering the *curses* program. The standard C library system(3) function is then called to exec the shell. When the shell dies, control is passed back to the *curses* program. The first thing the function does is reset the terminal driver back into an *in-curses* mode by calling resetty(). As we have learned, *curses* maintains information about each window in data structures (_win_st). We also know that *curses* has a good idea about what should be displayed on the terminal screen (curscr). However, if we mess up the terminal screen by passing control to some other process (the shell in this case), then *curses* has a false impression of what is really being displayed on the terminal screen. For this reason we call the function touchwin(). The purpose of touchwin() is to make *curses* think that the window needs to be fully updated (Chapter 1 goes into more detail about it). This causes the whole window to be redisplayed when wrefresh() is next called. We use touchwin() to update the curscr window. The purpose here is to force a clear-screen sequence to the terminal, while at the same time updating the terminal screen with any data that was displayed by *curses* before it passed control to the shell.

```
shell()
{
    savetty();

    reset_shell_mode();
    system("/bin/sh");
    resetty();
    touchwin(curscr);
    wrefresh(curscr);
}
```

4.15 Refreshing the terminal screen

The function `wrefresh(win)` has been discussed many times in the book so far. We know that its purpose is to copy a named window to the physical terminal screen, taking into account what has already been displayed there so that it can effectively optimize character output. We have also learned that the pseudo-function `refresh()` does the same thing, using the `stdscr` window as default. If you are maintaining several windows in your program, calling `wrefresh()` on each window is not a very efficient method of updating the terminal screen. To explain why this is so, here is an example of the function `wrefresh()`:

```
wrefresh(win)
WINDOW *win;
{
    wnoutrefresh(win);
    return(doupdate());
}
```

We know that *curses* keeps a record of two data structures representing the terminal screen: `curscr` — a data representation of the physical screen, and `stdscr` — a virtual screen representing what the programmer wants on the screen. The function `wnoutrefresh()` copies a named window to the virtual screen, and `doupdate()` updates the physical screen.

If you want to output several windows at the same time, calling `wrefresh()` on each consecutive window will result in many unnecessary calls to `wnoutrefresh()` and `doupdate()`. This updates the physical screen several times and will have an effect of separate bursts of output to the terminal screen as each window is individually displayed.

You can see, therefore, that it is better to call `wnoutrefresh()` for each window and then call `doupdate()` once only so that the physical screen receives one final update. This method will not only be faster in its execution, but will also reduce the amount of characters that have to be transmitted to the terminal to complete the physical update.

CHAPTER 5

Video attributes

Modern terminals often support some form of video attributes. These attributes are normally in the form of enabling characters to be displayed in some highlighted mode such as reverse video, or underlined, and so on. There are also many terminals that support more complex attributes such as color and the use of alternate character sets.

This chapter explains how *curses* manipulates video attributes and how you, the programmer, can use them.

5.1   What is a video attribute?

Almost all modern terminals nowadays support a set of video attributes, but what exactly is a video attribute? As far as *curses* is concerned, it is the capability to draw a character on the terminal screen in some way that makes it stand out differently from other characters being displayed. Characters in reverse video, for example, are displayed dark on a light background. This, by the way, is the default *highlight* mode.

As a character is added to a window with waddch(), its associated attributes are added with it (if they are set). For example, the character may be added to the window *underlined* and *blinking*.

Every *curses* window has a set of attributes associated with it. These attributes are said to be current attributes and are associated with each character as it is added to the window. Attributes remain the property of a character and stay with it as it is moved — for example, when it is shifted during insert or delete line or character operations, or when the window is scrolled or moved.

As long as the terminal supports a particular attribute, characters are displayed in this pseudo-graphic form on the terminal screen whenever they are requested to do so. It is a bit like being able to add characters to the screen with a paintbrush, where the attributes represent the colors of your paint.

However, not all terminals support all attributes. If *curses* finds that a particular requested attribute is not supported by the current terminal it attempts to find a substitute attribute. If no replacement seems available, *curses* will just ignore the request and no error is generated. It is important to realize that displaying characters with attributes in this way will only take effect on the screen if the terminal running the *curses* program can apply them, and of course they have to be specified in the terminal's terminfo description.

Attributes are represented by constants defined in the include file <curses.h>. These constants were introduced in the System V release of the package and are preceded by "A_". Attributes may be combined by *OR'ing* them together so that they can be turned on or off as required. They are as follows:

A_STANDOUT	*Curses* refers to this attribute as being the terminal's best highlight mode.
A_UNDERLINE	Characters are displayed on the screen underlined.
A_REVERSE	Characters are displayed inverse (dark on a bright background). This mode is often referred to as *reverse* or *inverse video* mode (often the same as A_STANDOUT).
A_BLINK	Characters added in this mode will blink on the screen. It is often referred to as *flash* mode.

A_DIM   Characters are displayed in *half-intensity* mode; normal
                 display characters seem brighter.

A_BOLD   Characters are displayed in *high-intensity* mode and are
                 brighter than normal, so that they stand out more than
                 characters displayed in A_STANDOUT.

A_NORMAL   Turns off all attributes; output is displayed at normal
                 intensity without underlining, blinking, bold, dim, or
                 reverse video.

The following two attributes are supported on both UNIX System V.2 and V.3
releases, but since they may change in the future it is not a good idea to depend
on them:

A_INVIS   Characters are concealed on the terminal screen although
                 they still exist within the WINDOW data structure.

A_PROTECT   Turns on *protect* mode and sets the terminal into *write-
                 protect* mode. Characters written in this mode are
                 protected from accidental erasure or change. Normally,
                 screen scrolling features of the terminal will not work
                 while the screen is in *write-protect* mode and the
                 terminal prohibits the cursor from entering into these
                 areas and forces the cursor to pass over them.

The following set of constants enable you to select individual parts of a character
in a window (see Section 4.7):

A_ATTRIBUTES   Used to extract the attributes part of a character.

A_CHARTEXT   Used to extract the text part of the character.

A_ALTCHARSET   If the terminal supports a line-drawing alternate
                 character set, this constant is used to toggle it on or off.

A_COLOR   If the terminal has color capabilities, this constant is used
                 to extract a color-pair from the attribute mask.

5.2 Setting attributes

A set of functions are provided specifically for turning attributes on and off.
These functions manipulate the WINDOW structure variable _attrs. As a
character is added to a window, the set attributes in _attrs are also *OR'ed* into
it.

Prior to the release of UNIX System V, the only attribute that *curses*
supported was *standout* mode. This mode was turned on by the function
wstandout(win) and off with wstandend(win). Both these functions still exist

within the *curses* package along with their `stdscr` macros `standout()` and `standend()`.

A major change that came about with the release of System V was better support for video attributes. The type `chtype` was introduced so that future enhancements to *curses* (which will no doubt include even more support for video attributes) will not conflict with *curses* programs written on earlier System V versions of the package. The idea is that if more attributes are added, then `chtype` is all that needs to be changed to accommodate the extra attributes. At present the supported attributes fit quite nicely into an unsigned short which is the type currently used for `chtype`, but don't depend on it — it may change in the future and could also be defined differently on your system.

Apart from `standout()` and `standend()`, a set of three functions is provided for manipulating video attributes. Incidentally, these functions could have been defined as pseudo-functions in `<curses.h>` but for some reason they have been implemented as real functions. There is no point in testing their return values as these functions always return `OK` even if the terminal does not support the attributes you are manipulating. The following list outlines these functions:

`wattrset(win,attrs)`   Sets the current attributes in window `win` to that given in `attrs`.

`wattron(win,attrs)`   Turns on the current attributes in window `win` to that given in `attrs`.

`wattroff(win,attrs)`   Turns off the attributes specified in `attrs` in the window `win`.

It is possible to combine attributes. For example, if you want to turn on bold and underline attributes, you just simply *OR* them together:

```
wattron(win, A_BOLD | A_UNDERLINE);
```

If you wish to turn off a specified attribute selectively, use `wattroff()`:

```
wattroff(win, A_BOLD);
```

To turn off all attributes in a window you can use `wattrset()`:

```
wattrset(win, A_NORMAL);
```

Of course, there is the usual support for `stdscr`. The pseudo-functions `attrset(attrs)`, `attron(attrs)` and `attroff(attrs)` are provided for this purpose. As an example of how to use these functions, the following program uses them to selectively turn attributes on and off:

```
#include <curses.h>

main()
{
        initscr();

        standout();
        mvaddstr(0,8,"this is using standout()");
        standend();
        attrset(A_STANDOUT);
        mvaddstr(2,8,"this is STANDOUT mode");
        attroff(A_STANDOUT);
        attron(A_REVERSE);
        mvaddstr(4,8,"this is REVERSE mode");
        attroff(A_REVERSE);
        attron(A_BOLD);
        mvaddstr(6,8,"this is BOLD mode");
        attroff(A_BOLD);
        attron(A_UNDERLINE);
        mvaddstr(8,8,"this is UNDERLINE mode");
        attroff(A_UNDERLINE);
        attron(A_DIM);
        mvaddstr(10,8,"this is DIM mode");
        attroff(A_DIM);
        attron(A_BLINK);
        mvaddstr(12,8,"this is BLINK mode");
        attroff(A_BLINK);
        attron(A_BOLD|A_UNDERLINE|A_BLINK);
        mvaddstr(14,8,"this is BOLD, UNDERLINED, BLINKING");
        attrset(A_NORMAL);
        mvaddstr(16,8,"This is INVISIBLE [");
        attron(A_INVIS);
        addstr("this text is invisible");
        attroff(A_INVIS);
        addch(']');
        attron(A_REVERSE|A_BLINK);
        mvaddstr(18,8,"this is REVERSE & BLINKING");
        attrset(A_NORMAL);
        mvaddstr(20,8,"this is NORMAL mode");
        attroff(A_NORMAL);
        refresh();
        endwin();
}
```

5.3 Using an alternative character set

Traditionally, *curses* has always used standard printable ASCII characters for output to the terminal screen, that is, characters whose hexadecimal values range from 20 through 7E. However, some terminals in response to a particular character sequence switch to an alternate character set. The characters in this alternate set are graphics characters or glyphs of some sort, often used for graphs, charts and other simple line-drawing figures. When this mode is enabled, the terminal responds differently to standard ASCII characters it receives: they are mapped to their graphic character representation. Sending **ASCII character 2**, for example, to a **Wyse 50** terminal when in *local-graphics-mode* makes the graphics character for a **top-left-hand-corner** '⌐' glyph appear on the terminal screen instead of the normal ASCII character 2.

Since the release of System V.3, *curses* supports the use of an alternate character set (ACS) by allowing you to use specially defined macros and constants provided in the <curses.h> include file. For example, there is a set of constants which provide a mechanism to index the acs_map[] array. This array contains a list of all the characters in the ACS set which are defined in the terminal's terminfo description. If the terminal description does not define a particular alternate character, then a default line-drawing character is used instead. The default ACS set used (see Table 5.1) is based on the **DEC VT100** and **Teletype 5420** alternate character set. The method of defining an alternate character set within the terminfo description is discussed in Chapter 8 (see Section 8.15).

To print a character that is part of the terminal's alternate character set, you choose the relevant macro prefixed with ACS_ and use it as an argument to waddch(). For example, ACS_ULCORNER is the macro for the *upper-left-corner* glyph. So long as the terminal has this glyph defined in its terminfo description, the character found in the acs_map will be *OR'ed* with A_ALTCHARSET and then added to the specified window. If there is no line-drawing character defined in the terminfo entry for the glyph, a default ASCII character is used instead; in this case the default character is +.

Currently, *curses* supports only a subset of the standard alternate character set. These are the line-drawing characters from the **DEC VT100** terminal, plus a few from the **Teletype 5420** (see Table 3). The ACS standard is still growing, so there may be support for newer line-drawing glyphs and non-line-drawing glyphs in the future.

Table 5.1: *Supported line-drawing character set.*

ACS LINE DRAWING CHARACTERS			
Constant	*Default*	*VT100 Character*	*Description*
ACS_ULCORNER	+	l	upper left corner
ACS_LLCORNER	+	m	lower left corner
ACS_URCORNER	+	k	upper right corner
ACS_LRCORNER	+	j	lower right corner
ACS_RTEE	+	u	right tee (⊣)
ACS_LTEE	+	t	left tee (⊢)
ACS_BTEE	+	v	bottom tee (⊥)
ACS_TTEE	+	w	top tee (⊤)
ACS_HLINE	-	q	horizontal line
ACS_VLINE	|	x	vertical line
ACS_PLUS	+	n	plus
ACS_S1	-	o	scan line 1
ACS_S9	_	s	scan line 9
ACS_DIAMOND	*	'	diamond
ACS_CKBOARD	:	a	checker board (stipple)
ACS_DEGREE	'	f	degree symbol
ACS_PLMINUS	#	g	plus/minus
ACS_BULLET	o	~	bullet
Constant	*Default*	*Teletype 5420 Character*	*Description*
ACS_LARROW	<	,	arrow pointing left
ACS_RARROW	>	+	arrow pointing right
ACS_DARROW	v	.	arrow pointing down
ACS_UARROW	^	-	arrow pointing up
ACS_BOARD	#	h	board of squares
ACS_LANTERN	#	i	lantern symbol
ACS_BLOCK	#	0	solid square block

Incidentally, the System V.2 <curses.h> include file defines A_ALTCHARSET although it was not until System V.3 that the acs_map[] line-drawing features were introduced. The major difference is that in the System V.2 release of *curses*, the `A_ALTCHARSET` constant is used to turn on a terminal's alternate character set by using `attron(A_ALTCHARSET)`. All this does is send the appropriate escape sequence out to the terminal to turn this mode on. There is no `asc_map[]` and so there are no predefined constants for the relevant line-drawing glyphs; obviously you have to know what characters to send to the terminal to get the glyph you want. This is all very well if you realize that your program will work only on the terminal you wrote the program for.

The following function `acsbox()` draws a box around the window which is passed to it as an argument. It uses the alternate character set to do this. However, it should be pointed out that on systems that support ACS the *curses* function `box()` automatically uses the ACS line drawing features, but `acsbox()` serves as a good example anyway:

```
acsbox(w)
WINDOW *w;
{
    register int y,x;

    wattron(w, A_ALTCHARSET);
    for(x = 1; x < w->_maxx - 1; x++) {
        mvwaddch(w, 0, x, ACS_HLINE);
        mvwaddch(w, w->_maxy - 1, x, ACS_HLINE);
    }
    for(y = 1; y < w->_maxy - 1; y++) {
        mvwaddch(w, y, 0, ACS_VLINE);
        mvwaddch(w, y, w->_maxx - 1, ACS_VLINE);
    }
    mvwaddch(w, 0, 0, ACS_ULCORNER);
    mvwaddch(w, 0, w->_maxx - 1, ACS_URCORNER);
    mvwaddch(w, w->_maxy - 1, 0, ACS_LLCORNER);
    mvwaddch(w, w->_maxy - 1, w->_maxx - 1, ACS_LRCORNER);
    wattroff(w, A_ALTCHARSET);
}
```

5.4 Color

With the release of UNIX System V.3 release 2, *curses* now provides color support. This is a totally new feature and it will probably be enhanced further in later releases.

In *curses*, color attributes are always specified in pairs. This introduces a new buzz word: **color-pair**. A color-pair specifies a foreground color and a background color. The foreground color is the one that characters will be displayed in, and the background color is what the rest of the terminal screen will take on. If color is not used, the foreground is normally white and the background is black.

The *curses* support for color is based on the two most common color manipulation methods: the Hewlett Packard and the Tektronix methods. The Tektronix method is based on a set of 8 colors which can be used to select background or foreground colors independently, so that 64 different color pairs can be displayed at the same time.

With the Hewlett Packard method it is not possible to set either of the background or foreground colors independently. This method requires that 2 colors (a color-pair) are to be defined together at the same time. This means that out of 8 colors there are only 16 permutations of color pairs that can be displayed on the screen at the same time.

To start with, you must issue a call to `start_color()`. The most common place for this is straight after issuing a call to `initscr()` or somewhere soon after it, at the beginning stages of the program. This sets up the color environment within *curses*. `start_color()` initializes 8 colors which have symbolic constants defined in `<curses.h>`. These color constants all begin with `COLOR_`. The colors currently supported are black, blue, green, cyan, red, magenta, yellow and white. For example, the color constant for green is defined as `COLOR_GREEN`. This routine also initializes two variables also defined in `<curses.h>` — `COLORS` and `COLOR_PAIRS`. They are used to contain the maximum number of colors and the maximum number of color pairs that the terminal supports. Finally, this routine sets the terminal into its default color-pair. If the terminal does not support color then `ERR` is returned, but remember that even if the terminal does support color, if it has not been set up in the terminfo description then `ERR` will be returned anyway.

To use color, a special macro has been defined in `<curses.h>` so that you can manipulate color attributes as you would for any other attribute. The macro is called `COLOR_PAIR(n)`, where n specifies the color-pair to use. You can actually combine color attributes using the C logical operators with any of the other video attributes by using functions such as `attrset()` or `wattron()`. But before you use a color-pair, you must initialize it. You do this with `init_pair(pair, foreground, background)`. This function takes three arguments, the first being the pair number. This number can be any number between 1 and `COLOR_PAIRS` −1. The arguments `foreground` and `background` set up the color scheme for the pair; their values can be between 0 and `COLORS` −1. Once the color-pair has been set up with `init_pair()`, you actuate the colors with `wattron()`:

```
wattron(win,A_UNDERLINE | COLOR_PAIR(1));
```

This example actuates color-pair 1 and the underline attribute at the same time. From now on, any characters added to the window will be displayed in the background and foreground colors specified for the color-pair and underlined. Any of the functions used to set or modify attributes can be used with

COLOR_PAIR().

Another interesting function is init_color(color, red, green, blue), which modifies the definition of the color specified. The value of the first argument must be between 0 and COLORS −1. The arguments red, green and blue are values between 0 and 1000 which specify the RGB color components. Of course, this is only possible if the terminal is capable of changing color definitions. You can use the function can_change_color() to find out if it can: it returns TRUE if the terminal supports colors and they are changeable, otherwise FALSE is returned. If you only want to find out if the terminal supports colors you can use has_colors(). Once again this returns TRUE if it does, or else it returns FALSE.

To find out what the current color settings are, two more functions are provided. The function color_content(color, &red, &green, &blue) stores at these addresses the current color component values of color. The other function is pair_content(pair, &foreground, &background) which stores at these addresses the current color settings of a specified color-pair.

The following program demonstrates an example of color use:

```
/*
 * Curses color support
 * demonstration
 */
#include <curses.h>

int f,b,R,G,B;

#define FORGROUND 1
#define BACKGROUND 0

main(argc,argv)
int argc;
char *argv;
{
    initscr();
    keypad(stdscr,TRUE);
    cbreak();
    noecho();
    scrollok(stdscr,TRUE);

    if(!has_colors()) {
        endwin();
        fprintf(stderr,"\ncolor not supported\n");
        exit(1);
    }
```

```
    start_color();
    init_pair(1,COLOR_WHITE,COLOR_BLACK);
    attron(COLOR_PAIR(1));

    process();
    endwin();
    return(0);
}

fillwin()
{
    register int y,x;

    move(0,0);
    for(y = 0; y < LINES; y++)
        for(x = 0; x < COLS; x++)
            addch(' ');
}


process()
{

    while(1) {
        fillwin();
        mvprintw(10,15,"Function keys are:");
        mvprintw(12,15,"F1 = Set Foreground");
        mvprintw(13,15,"F2 = Set Background");
        mvprintw(14,15,"F3 = Modify RED content");
        mvprintw(15,15,"F4 = Modify GREEN content");
        mvprintw(16,15,"F5 = Modify BLUE content");
        mvprintw(18,15,"F8 = Quit program");
        refresh();
        switch(getch()) {
        case KEY_F(1):
            setfb(FORGROUND);
            break;
        case KEY_F(2):
            setfb(BACKGROUND);
            break;
        case KEY_F(3):
            modf(COLOR_RED);
            break;
        case KEY_F(4):
```

```
            modf(COLOR_GREEN);
            break;
        case KEY_F(5):
            modf(COLOR_BLUE);
            break;
        case KEY_F(8):
            return;
        default:
            beep();
        }
    }
}


/*
 * set foreground
 */
setfb(setting)
char setting;
{
    fillwin();
    mvprintw(12,10,"Use KEY_LEFT, KEY_RIGHT");
    mvprintw(13,10,"F1 to select");
    refresh();
    while(1) {
        switch(getch()) {
        case KEY_LEFT:
            if(setting == FORGROUND)
                f = f == 0 ? COLORS - 1: f - 1;
            else
                b = b == 0 ? COLORS - 1: b - 1;
            break;
        case KEY_RIGHT:
            if(setting == FORGROUND)
                f = f == COLORS - 1 ? 0: f + 1;
            else
                b = b == COLORS - 1 ? 0: b + 1;
            break;
        case KEY_F(1):
            return;
        default:
            beep();
        }
        init_pair(1,f,b);
```

```
    }
}

modf(setting)
int setting;
{
    if(!can_change_color()) {
        beep();
        return;
    }

    fillwin();
    mvprintw(12,10,"Use KEY_LEFT, KEY_RIGHT");
    mvprintw(13,10,"F1 to select");
    refresh();
    while(1) {
        switch(getch()) {
        case KEY_LEFT:
            if(setting == COLOR_RED)
                R = R == 0 ? 1000: R - 1;
            else if(setting == COLOR_GREEN)
                G = G == 0 ? 1000: G - 1;
            else
                B = B == 0 ? 1000: B - 1;
            break;
        case KEY_RIGHT:
            if(setting == COLOR_RED)
                R = R == 1000 ? 0: R + 1;
            else if(setting == COLOR_GREEN)
                G = G == 1000 ? 0: G + 1;
            else
                B = B == 1000 ? 0: B + 1;
            break;
        case KEY_F(1):
            return;
        default:
            beep();
        }
        init_color(f,R,G,B);
    }
}
```

5.5 Getting the attention of the user

Two functions which can be either useful or annoying, depending on the context of the program, are `flash()` and `beep()`. The function `flash()` tries to cause the screen to flash; it is intended to be a replacement for a bell and in fact calls `beep()` to sound the bell if it finds that it cannot flash. Similarly, `beep()` makes a bell sound. If for some reason the terminal cannot beep but can flash, then flash is used in its place. Both of these functions have been designed to attract the attention of the user. Since these functions use specific attributes of the terminal, this section is the appropriate place to describe them.

5.6 Soft labels

System V.3 also saw the introduction of soft-label support (sometimes called the function key line). It is a set of labels placed at the bottom of the screen which you can program to give a user-friendly look to your programs. It is especially handy if you are writing an editor, for example.

To manage soft labels, *curses* reduces the size of `stdscr` by 1 line and reserves it for use by the *curses* soft-label functions. Soft labels are optional, but if you decide to use them there are some rules concerned.

On a terminal supporting built-in soft labels, *curses* will use this feature, but if your terminal does not provide it *curses* will simulate it with software.

As mentioned previously, *curses* reduces the size of `stdscr` by 1 line and it also reduces the `LINES` variable. Since most terminals that support soft labels have 8 labels, *curses* has followed the same standard. Each label is 8 characters wide and the size of the string that will be put on a label is restricted to this size.

To use soft labels, the routine `slk_init(format)` must be called before calling `newterm()`. Because `initscr()` calls `newterm()` internally, you must also issue a call to `slk_init()` before calling this function. So, the normal place for this function to be called is at the beginning of your *curses* program just before calling `initscr()`.

Once *curses* has decided that the terminal does not support built-in soft labels, it realigns `stdscr` so that software soft-label emulation can be done. If software emulation is imminent, the argument `format` determines which format to use to build the soft labels on the screen. If `format` is 0 then labels are arranged in a 3-2-3 arrangement across the bottom line of the screen (see Figure 5.1). However, if `format` is 1, then the arrangement is 4-4 (see Figure 5.2).

To set up a soft-label, you use `slk_set(labelnum,label,format)`. The argument `labelnum` is the number of the label to set up, which is between 1 and 8. `label` is the string to place into (or put on) the label. It must be no more than 8 characters wide. If this argument is a `NULL` pointer then the label is filled with blanks. The `format` is either 0,1 or 2; this specifies how the data in the label is to be formatted. The format is left justified, centered or right justified, respectively.

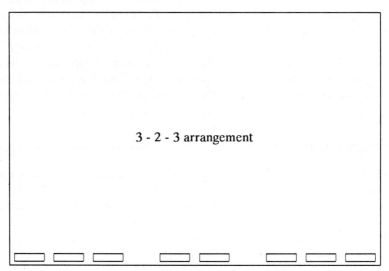

Figure 5.1

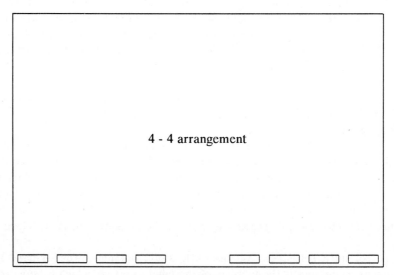

Figure 5.2

To find out what is currently in a label, the function slk_label(labelnum) is
provided. It returns a pointer to a character string holding the contents of the

label. The contents are not justified or centered and are handed back just as they were put on. You specify which label you want by placing the label number in the argument labelnum.

Two routines are provided to *refresh* the soft labels. The routine slk_noutrefresh() just calls wnoutrefresh() on the window. You normally use this to update each individual label, then call slk_refresh() to finally cause the physical update on the screen. These two functions work in a similar manner to wnoutrefresh() and doupdate() and in fact actually call these routines internally.

Other soft-label support routines are slk_clear(), slk_restore() and slk_touch(). The labels are cleared from the screen, restored after a slk_clear(), and touched so that all the labels are forced to be updated at the next call to slk_refresh().

This program sets up soft labels on the screen. Since it is just an example program, no command line checking is done.

```
#include <curses.h>

main(argc,argv)
int argc;
char *argv[];
{
    /*
     * command line argument is "0" for 3-2-3
     * or "1" for 4-4 arrangement.
     */
    slk_init(atoi(argv[1]));

    initscr();
    slk_set(1,"Insert",1);
    slk_set(2,"Quit",1);
    slk_set(3,"Add",1);
    slk_set(4,"Delete",1);
    slk_set(5,"Shell",1);
    slk_set(6,"Undo",1);
    slk_set(7,"Replace",1);
    slk_set(8,"Search",1);
    slk_touch();
    slk_refresh();
    move(0,0);
    getch();
    endwin();
}
```

CHAPTER 6

Using pads

So far we have discussed windows that have been restricted to the size of the terminal screen, and for most programs this is quite sufficient. However, a window can be of any reasonable size. *Curses* uses **pads** to manipulate windows that do not fit on the screen, and a set of routines for manipulating them is provided. This chapter explains how to use pads and what steps are necessary to manipulate them.

6.1 Manipulating a big window

The function newwin() returns a pointer to a new window whose dimensions are specified by its given arguments. The window returned will never be bigger than the values LINES and COLS, normally defined as being the dimensions of the terminal screen.

Whenever a large window was required in pre-System V versions of *curses*, it was necessary to create individual windows and manipulate them as if they were connected together on a grid. When a portion of the grid was to be displayed, the relevant window containing this portion was touched and refreshed, overlaying what was previously displayed. Program design was complex and slow at runtime.

Pads were introduced to overcome these problems. A pad is a WINDOW, but its size is not restricted to the size of the terminal screen, although only a portion of the window is displayed on the screen — the current portion of the pad being manipulated.

Any *curses* routine may be used with pads except for subwin(), wrefresh() and wnoutrefresh(). These are replaced with subpad(), prefresh() and pnoutrefresh().

To create a pad you use newpad(). To create a sub-window within a pad you use subpad(). Both of these functions return a pointer to a WINDOW.

The function newpad(lines,cols) resembles newwin() in that it creates a window, the size of which is defined by arguments lines and cols. To refresh a pad, it is necessary to use prefresh(). Using wrefresh() with a pad is illegal and may cause a core dump. Unlike windows created with newwin(), the size of a new pad is restricted only to the amount of memory available to the program. The pad may not necessarily be associated with a particular part of the screen (see Figure 6.1). Also, it is important to realize that pads are not automatically refreshed (i.e. from scrolling).

The function subpad(parentpad,lines,cols,begy,begx) is similar to subwin() except that it creates a sub-window (instead of a pad) within an existing parent pad. The subpad is lines by cols in size and its beginning coordinates are specified in begy and begx. Unlike subwin(), which returns a window whose **HOME** coordinates are always 0,0, subpad() returns a window which has **HOME** coordinates within the pad set by begy and begx. The new window is placed within the parent pad; changes to either the subpad or the parent pad will affect them both. If you want to refresh a subpad you should use touchwin() before using prefresh() on it. Incidentally, subpad() was introduced with UNIX System V.3.

The function prefresh(pad,ptopy,ptopx,sminy,sminx,smaxy,smaxx) functions the same way on pads as wrefresh() does on windows. The extra arguments are needed so that *curses* can compute which part of the pad is to be displayed and whereabouts on the terminal screen it is to be placed.

ptopy and ptopx specify the upper left corner of the rectangular portion of the pad to be displayed. These coordinates are with respect to the pads **HOME** coordinates which are the same as those of an ordinary window: begy = 0, begx = 0.

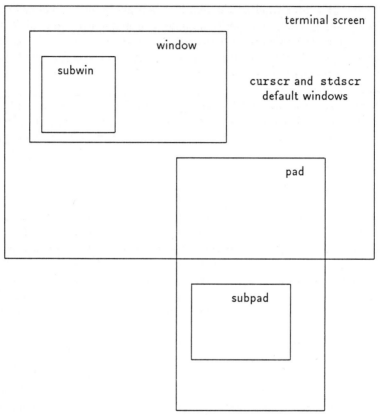

Figure 6.1

sminy and sminx specify the y,x coordinates of the terminal screen where the upper left-hand corner of the portion of the pad to be displayed will be placed.

smaxy and smaxx specify the maximum y,x coordinates of the terminal screen where display output will occur. You must make sure that the rectangular portion of the pad to be displayed will fit within the bounds of stdscr. The arguments passed to prefresh() are validated; negative values are set to zero, and values overlapping the maximum size of the screen are truncated so that it fits what it can on the screen.

pnoutrefresh(pad,ptopy,ptopx,sminy,sminx,smaxy,smaxx) is similar to wnoutrefresh(), and its arguments are the same as prefresh(). In fact,

this function is called by prefresh(), passing the very same arguments to
pnoutrefresh(). Here is an example of prefresh():

```
prefresh(pad,ptopy,ptopx,sminy,sminx,smaxy,smaxx)
WINDOW *pad;
int ptopy,ptopx,sminy,sminx,smaxy,smaxx;
{
    pnoutrefresh(pad,ptopy,ptopx,sminy,sminx,smaxy,smaxx);
    return(doupdate());
}
```

To clarify this we will study a simple program which uses both a pad and a
window:

```
#include <curses.h>

main()
{
    WINDOW *pad, *win;
    chtype c;

    initscr();
    noecho();
    raw();

    pad = newpad(50,50);
    win = newwin(5,50,15,25);
    scrollok(win,TRUE);

    while((c = getch()) != 'Z') {
        waddch(pad,c);
        waddch(win,c);
        wrefresh(win);
    }
    prefresh(pad,0,0,5,5,10,40);
    endwin();
}
```

We first initialize *curses* with initscr(). All echoing is done within the
program, so echo is turned off with noecho(). We arrange the *tty* driver so that
characters are returned to the program immediately they are typed. This is done
by raw().

Two windows are created, the first of which is a pad. The pad's dimensions
are 50 lines in height and 50 columns in width. The window's dimensions are 5

lines in height and 50 columns in width and it is placed in relation to `stdscr` at coordinates `begy = 15, begx = 25`. Scrolling is then set to `TRUE` on the window, allowing it to scroll legally.

The program is then placed into a loop awaiting keyboard input with `getch()`, the loop terminating on an **Upper-case Z**. Within the loop each character received is added to both pad and window, but only the window is refreshed. So, as characters are entered at the keyboard they will be displayed only within the window.

After the terminating character is detected the loop terminates and `prefresh()` is called to update the portion of the pad on the screen.

The arguments to `prefresh()` specify that the portion of the pad to be displayed starts from 0,0 within the pad; this is the top left-hand corner of the rectangle to be displayed. The arguments 5,5 specify that the portion of the pad to display is placed on the screen at line 5, column 5. The last two arguments specify that the contents of the portion of the pad to output is cut off at line 10 and column 40 of the screen. This means that since the pad starts at line 5 and is restricted to line 10, the total number of lines displayed from within the pad is calculated as:

$$display\_lines = (10 - 5) + 1$$

Similarly, since the pad starts at column 5 and is restricted to column 40, the total number of columns displayed from within the pad is computed as:

$$display\_columns = (40 - 5) + 1$$

The addition of 1 to both formulae is because windows start from 0,0. The end result displays a rectangular portion of pad 6 lines in height and 36 columns wide, the portion being taken from the very top corner of the pad.

CHAPTER 7

Building terminfo descriptions

"Terminfo's mystique is *usually* left for those that are magical !"

— anon.

To cover terminfo entirely would require a separate text on the subject as it is a huge topic and can be extremely complex, but no book about *curses* would be complete without a chapter on terminfo. For this reason, terminfo is discussed in this chapter with enough detail to allow you to understand and use it.

7.1 What is terminfo?

Terminals come in all shapes and sizes. Some are more clever than others. There are dumb terminals as well as smart ones, some support alternate character sets and others don't, some have large screens, others small, and so on.

Terminfo is a database of terminal capabilities. The database consists of a set of binary files created by the UNIX command **tic**. **Tic** takes a text file containing a description of a terminal and compiles it into binary form. Each file contains a description of a particular terminal's capabilities which can be accessed from within a C program by using a set of low-level terminfo routines.

Terminfo is used by many UNIX programs which manipulate the terminal screen — for example, **vi, more** and **tput**. Games such as **aliens, hack** and **rogue** use terminfo, and of course *curses* uses terminfo extensively. At the low level, *curses* uses the terminfo routines in a controlled manner. That is, *curses* is a platform of screen management routines that sits on top of the low-level terminfo platform.

Many features which terminfo needs to manipulate a terminal are provided in the terminal's hardware or firmware. It is possible to just repaint the terminal screen every time there is a change to be made, but it is more efficient to use the supported features of the terminal. The problem is that most terminals differ in their capabilities. Even if similar capabilities are supported, different operations are almost always required. This is why it is necessary to have a database of individual terminal descriptions, each defining the hardware-dependent sequences of instructions needed to perform an operation.

To determine which description in the database to use, terminfo requires the shell environment variable **TERM** to be defined. This tells terminfo what type of terminal it is using.

The compiled files are in the directory /usr/lib/terminfo (see Section 2.2). The only user who can modify this directory structure is super-user. Therefore, if you need to modify or install a new terminfo database entry, you will have to ask the system supervisor or system administrator to install it for you. Before you do this, try out your new or modified description first to make sure that it is working correctly.

For the rest of this chapter we will assume that we are working with a generic **ansi** terminal. The following is typical of what you would go through to modify a terminfo database description.

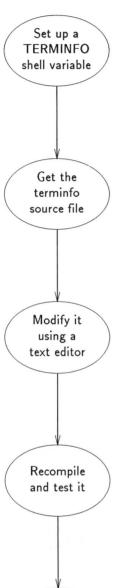

Terminfo by default looks in the directory **/usr/lib/terminfo** for its database of terminal descriptions. but you can override this by defining a shell environment variable — **TERMINFO** (see Section 2.3). This tells terminfo to look there instead. This would normally be a directory in your home directory.

You issue the command **infocmp -I** or **untic** to obtain the text based source description of the terminal you are using. You can redirect the output to a file of your choice. These files are historically called *.ti* files so, for example, for the ansi terminal you could create the file *ansi.ti*.

Now that you have the source description file, you can modify its contents using your favorite text editor. The next section describes the format of these files in detail.

You use the **tic** command to compile a source description file. The compiled description file is automatically placed in the directory tree which you set up in the **TERMINFO** shell variable. You can now test the description to make sure it is working correctly.

If the description is working, you can hand over the source description file to the system administrator, who will install it for you.

7.2 Terminfo description file format

A terminfo description contains several fields, with each field separated by a comma. Any spaces or tabs (or any white space) is ignored between the ending comma of a field and the beginning of the next description field.

Comments may be placed into a terminfo description file by placing the pound or hash '#' character at the beginning of a line. A line beginning with this character is ignored and will not form part of the compiled description. However, you cannot place comments within the body of a description: if you want to put a comment in a description file, you must place it on a separate line beginning with a pound character. The best places for comments are at the beginning of the file before the description, or at the end of the file after it.

It is sometimes necessary to comment out a particular description field. To do this you may place a period character '.' before the capability description name. The following terminfo description is for an ansi terminal. As an example, the capability for function key 1 (capability kf1) has been commented out by placing a period before it.

```
#
# Terminfo description file for a generic ansi terminal
#
ansi|ANSI|Generic Ansi Standard Terminal,
        am, xon,
        cols#80, lines#24,
        bel=^G, blink=\E[5m, bold=\E[1m, cbt=\E[Z,
        clear=\E[H\E[J, cr=\r, cub=\E[%p1%dD, cub1=\b,
        cud=\E[%p1%dB, cud1=\n, cuf=\E[%p1%dC, cuf1=\E[C,
        cup=\E[%i%p1%d;%p2%dH, cuu=\E[%p1%dA, cuu1=\E[A,
        dch1=\E[P, dl=\E[%p1%dM, dl1=\E[M, ed=\E[J, el=\E[K,
        home=\E[H, hpa=\E[%p1%{1}%+%dG, ht=\t, hts=\EH,
        ich=\E[%p1%d@, ich1=\E[@, il=\E[%p1%dL, il1=\E[L,
        ind=\n, invis=\E[8m, kbs=\b, kcub1=\E[D, kcud1=\E[B,
        kcuf1=\E[C, kcuu1=\E[A, khome=\E[H,
        kend=\E[Y, .kf1=EOP, kf10=\EOY, kf11=\EOZ,
        kf12=\EOA, kf2=\EOQ, kf3=\EOR, kf4=\EOS, kf5=\EOT,
        kf6=\EOU, kf7=\EOV, kf8=\EOW, kf9=\EOX,
        rep=%p1%c\E[%p2%{1}%-%db, rev=\E[7m, rmso=\E[m,
        rmul=\E[m,
        sgr=\E[%?%p1%t7;%;%?%p2%t4;%;%?%p3%t7;%;%?%p4%t5;%;%?%p6%t1;%;m,
        sgr0=\E[0m, smso=\E[7m, smul=\E[4m, tbc=\E[2g,
        vpa=\E[%p1%{1}%+%dd,
#
# End of description
#
```

Note how the description lines are indented. Lines that are part of the description file (apart from comments and the terminal name line) must be preceded by white space. A tab character is usually used.

The first line of the description contains the terminal name, alias names, and a short description of the terminal type. Each name or alias name is separated by the bar character '|', but none of these except the last one should contain any white space characters.

The first name is the name most commonly used to set the **TERM** environment variable. Any other names are known as *aliases*. You may use one of these names, if you wish, in place of the first name for **TERM**; it does not really matter. The last name given is normally a verbose description of the terminal described. It is not mandatory, but makes the description more understandable.

Any amount of alias names can be specified except that all names must be unique within the first 14 characters and the whole line must not exceed 128 characters in total.

Names that are chosen for the terminal including alias names should give some idea of the terminal type. Assuming there is more than one name for the terminal, each name should start with a common root name. A typical root name would not contain any odd characters such as the hyphen character '-', and it should be distinguishable from any specified alias names.

If there are any special preferred hardware modes that you prefer to use then these should be shown by appending a hyphen '-' and the type of mode to the end of the root name. For example, the previous terminfo description is for a plain generic type ansi terminal, but supposing you flick a switch on the back of the terminal because you want to use the 25-line mode: you will now want to build a similar terminfo entry for an ansi terminal with 25 lines. One way you could do this is to copy the generic ansi description to a file named *ansi-25.ti*, modify the capability `lines#` to 25, and change the name's description line to reflect the new terminfo entry. This is what the new file would look like:

```
#
# Terminfo description file for a generic ansi terminal
# with a 25 line screen
#
ansi-25|ANSI-25|Generic 25 Line Ansi Standard Terminal,
        am, xon,
        cols#80, lines#25,
        bel=^G, blink=\E[5m, bold=\E[1m, cbt=\E[Z,
        clear=\E[H\E[J, cr=\r, cub=\E[%p1%dD, cub1=\b,
        cud=\E[%p1%dB, cud1=\n, cuf=\E[%p1%dC, cuf1=\E[C,
        cup=\E[%i%p1%d;%p2%dH, cuu=\E[%p1%dA, cuu1=\E[A,
        dch1=\E[P, dl=\E[%p1%dM, dl1=\E[M, ed=\E[J, el=\E[K,
```

```
        home=\E[H, hpa=\E[%p1%{1}%+%dG, ht=\t, hts=\EH,
        ich=\E[%p1%d@, ich1=\E[@, il=\E[%p1%dL, il1=\E[L,
        ind=\n, invis=\E[8m, kbs=\b, kcub1=\E[D, kcud1=\E[B,
        kcuf1=\E[C, kcuu1=\E[A, khome=\E[H,
        kend=\E[Y, .kf1=EOP, kf10=\EOY, kf11=\EOZ,
        kf12=\EOA, kf2=\EOQ, kf3=\EOR, kf4=\EOS, kf5=\EOT,
        kf6=\EOU, kf7=\EOV, kf8=\EOW, kf9=\EOX,
        rep=%p1%c\E[%p2%{1}%-%db, rev=\E[7m, rmso=\E[m,
        rmul=\E[m,
        sgr=\E[%?%p1%t7;%;%?%p2%t4;%;%?%p3%t7;%;%?%p4%t5;%;%?%p6%t1;%;m,
        sgr0=\E[0m, smso=\E[7m, smul=\E[4m, tbc=\E[2g,
        vpa=\E[%p1%{1}%+%dd,
#
# End of description
#
```

There is a special capability which you can use for this purpose. If there are two or more similar terminals, one terminal can be defined in such a way that it uses another terminal's description. The capability use is an instruction to use another terminal's terminfo description, and more than one use capability can be specified in the same description. Capabilities which are described before use in the description file override those in the referred description. Therefore, the description file *ansi-25.ti* would be better written like this:

```
#
# Terminfo description file for a generic ansi terminal
# with a 25 line screen
#
ansi-25|ANSI-25|Generic 25 Line Ansi Standard Terminal,
        lines#25, use=ansi,
#
# End of description
#
```

This example says to use the description for the generic ansi terminal, except for the capability lines which is described here.

You can also cancel out a capability in the referred terminal description, if you don't want to include its definition. If, for example, the terminal does not support a capability defined within the referred description, you need to omit its definition. You can do this by placing the at '@' character to the right of the capability to be canceled, just before its definition.

For example, the following description cancels the blink capability but includes all others in the ansi description except lines.

```
#
# Terminfo description file for a generic ansi terminal
# with a 25 line screen without blink mode
#
ansi-25|ANSI-25|Generic 25 Line Ansi Standard Terminal-No blink,
        lines#25,  blink@,  use=ansi,
#
# End of description
#
```

Table 7.1

TERMINAL NAMING CONVENTION		
Suffix	*Description*	*Example*
-w	Wide screen (greater than 80 columns)	ansi-w
-am	Terminal with automatic margins (default)	ansi-am
-nam	Terminal has no automatic margins	ansi-nam
-l	Number of lines on the screen (example = 25)	ansi-25
-xc	Number of columns across the screen	ansi-x132
-lxc	Number of both lines and columns	ansi-26x132
-na	Arrow keys are only supported in local mode	ansi-na
-np	Number of pages in local memory (example = 4)	ansi-4p
-rv	Terminal operates normally in reverse video mode	ansi-rv
-s	Terminal has optional status line enabled	ansi-s

A common naming convention exists for naming terminals. Table 7.1 outlines terminfo name suffixes which should be appended to the root name when necessary. The root name *ansi* has been used for this example.

7.3 Compiling a description

Assuming you have *write* permission in the /usr/lib/terminfo directory, you use the program **tic** to compile the source description file. For the *ansi-25.ti* file, tic would place the compiled description file in the directory /usr/lib/terminfo/a. So, the complete path name for this compiled terminfo description would be /usr/lib/terminfo/a/ansi-25. Since we have created an alias name (ANSI-25 in the description file) for this description, tic will link the compiled file to the file /usr/lib/terminfo/A/ANSI-25. Aliases are implemented by multiple links to the compiled master description.

7.4 Creating a description

Before you attempt to create a new terminal description you should consider trying to obtain one from someone else who might use the same or similar terminal on a UNIX machine. Try contacting the manufacturer or distributor of the terminal, in case they have already created a description file. They should at least be able to direct you to any of their clients who might have a UNIX system and would have faced similar problems. Other good sources are bulletin boards, local university computer departments, magazines and UNIX user groups. If all else fails, try to find out if another terminal has similar capabilities and modify that to suit your terminal.

If the terminal has some exceptionally odd capabilities, it just may be that even terminfo cannot use it. It is wise to try and find out how the terminal behaves before purchasing it.

The best way to create a terminal description file is not to. Start by choosing a terminal that is already supported by your UNIX system, and you will save yourself a lot of trouble. However, if you have to build a terminal description file from scratch, the best place to start is with the manufacturer's owner's manual. This should provide you with enough information to at least get the terminal working to some degree. It's a good idea to start with the capabilities which are common to most terminals, and work on from there. For example, you should be able to figure out how many lines and columns the terminal has.

After compiling your new description, you can test it by using one of the UNIX support programs which uses terminfo or *curses*. The best test, though, is *vi*. If *vi* works properly in visual mode, then you have mastered the art of creating a terminfo description. *Vi*, however, needs only a basic set of capabilities defined for visual mode. Table 7.2 lists the minimum set of capabilities needed for **vi** to work.

The program *infocmp* is used to uncompile a description. This program was introduced with UNIX System V.3. If you do not have *infocmp*, try to obtain *untic*, a similar program in the public domain. These programs are useful during the testing and building stages of a terminfo description. The output of either can be used directly as input to *tic*, so you can use them to extract a description for modification.

Infocmp has many useful runtime switches, and your UNIX reference manual will give you more information. Generally, entering the command at the UNIX prompt without an argument will print the terminal description which is set up in your **TERM** environment variable; if you specify the name of a terminal as an argument to *infocmp*, it will print that terminal's description file instead.

Table 7.2

MINIMUM *vi* TERMINAL CAPABILITY REQUIREMENTS			
Type	*Cap-name*	*Variable*	*Description*
string	cup	`cursor_address`	Move to row y column x
string	cuu1	`cursor_up`	Move cursor up 1 line
string	clear	`clear_screen`	Clear screen & home cursor
string	ind	`scroll_forward`	Scroll text up
string	cr	`carriage_return`	Carriage return
numeric	lines	`lines`	Number of lines on screen
numeric	cols	`columns`	Number of columns on a line

While you are testing a new description, it's a good idea to set the terminal and *tty* driver into a low baud rate. This way you can watch how the terminal reacts to the defined capabilities, and you can often detect where your problem is. To do this, use the *stty* command to reset the baud rate to, say, 300 or less if possible; set up the terminal so that it operates at this new speed, then edit a temporary file with *vi*. Pay special attention to how *vi* reacts in *insert* mode.

7.5 Defining capabilities

The description of terminal capabilities starts after the initial line containing the name and alias names of the terminal to be described. These lines are indented to distinguish them from alias name and comment lines. It does not matter how many capabilities you place on a line but it is not good practice to cause a line to overlap. Try to keep the description file readable. In general, a capability should be no longer than 128 characters including its capability name. Each capability is separated by a comma, including the last capability on the line. There are three types of capability, as follows:

Boolean   These capabilities specify that a terminal supports some particular feature (or bug). If the feature is supported, then the capability should be defined. For example, most terminals support X-on/X-off handshaking. This can be specified by defining xon in the description.

Numeric   Numeric capabilities specify the size of a particular feature. For example, you can specify the physical size of the screen by defining capabilities lines and cols.

String   These capabilities specify the sequence of characters necessary to make the terminal perform a particular operation. For example, sending the escape sequence "\E[H" to an ansi terminal makes the cursor return to its **home** position, which is the top left-hand corner. This is specified by the string capability home as home=\E[H,. Note the comma at the end of the description.

A terminal description contains abbreviated capability names, fashioned after the ANSI X3.64 1979 specification standard. A C-programmer can access these capabilities at the terminfo level by cross-referencing the abbreviated names with a set of defined variables in the <term.h> include file. The term most often used for an abbreviated capability name is *capname*. Capnames will be explained later.

To assign a number to a numeric capability you must use the pound '#' character. For example, lines#24 specifies that the terminal has 24 lines. String variables use the equals '=' character for assignment, home=\E[H for example.

Within a string capability definition it is often necessary to specify a non-printable character which forms part of the string sequence. These characters adopt the C escape backslash '\' notation. For example, the aforementioned ansi description specifies the string capability cr to be defined as cr=\r. The notation \r is actually the C-language representation of the ASCII carriage return character. This notation is referred to as *escaping*.

Characters that have special meaning to the terminfo compiler *tic* are also escaped. For example, the comma is used for a description field separator, so if it is to be used in a string definition, it should be distinguished in some way. To do this, prepend the comma with a backslash: \,.

Characters can also be specified as an octal number — a three-digit octal number specified after a backslash. For example, you could specify \040 which represents the octal value for an ASCII space character.

A special notation for control characters is also adopted. The carat or hat character '^' is prepended to a normal upper-case character, so the notation ^Z means Control-Z; similarly, the notation ^X means Control-X.

Table 7.3 outlines the notations often used to replace certain characters in a string definition.

Table 7.3

CHARACTER NOTATIONS	
Sequence	*Character*
\E	ESCAPE
\e	ESCAPE
\n	New-line
\l	Linefeed
\r	Carriage Return
\t	Tab
\b	Backspace
\f	Formfeed
\s	Space
\,	Comma
\\	Backslash
\^	Carat
\:	Colon
\0	Null or Pad
\123	Octal number
^X	Control-X

7.6 Padding

Certain terminals require padding or "no-operation" commands so that they can execute the commands they have just received. Certain commands that are sent to a terminal are complex and the terminal needs time (usually only a couple of milliseconds) to digest them before continuing with the next. During this period, when the terminal cannot respond to other commands that may have been sent, padding characters are sent to the terminal. These characters (usually nulls) are in effect "no-op" instructions and the terminal ignores them. This gives the terminal enough time to complete its last instruction. This is normally done by the hardware X-on/X-off handshaking but is sometimes required for certain other operations.

To specify padding the notation $<n>$ is used, where n represents the required time delay in milliseconds. The delay time may be specified as either a whole number or a number to 1 decimal place. For example, $<6>$ and $<10.5>$ are legal padding specifications, but $<3.35>$ is not. A number may be followed by either one or both characters '*' and '/' depending on the padding required. The '*' character implies that the padding delay required will be proportional to the number of lines which will be affected by the operation, so that the specified delay is the effective unit of padding required per line. The '/' character implies that padding is mandatory. This means that padding is done regardless of X-on/X-off handshaking.

It is important to realize that transmitting pad characters can slow the terminal down, and can sometimes induce unnecessary loading of the system. Therefore, you should consult your terminal documentation for the correct padding requirements of the terminal.

7.7 Parameterized arguments in strings

At run time, some string capabilities require parameterized arguments. This is true for most terminals, especially cursor-addressing capabilities.

Take, for example, the ansi terminal. The string sequence to move the cursor to line 10, column 8 is \E[10;8H. But how does one define this string in the terminfo description so that terminfo will send the real required line and column addresses at runtime? Obviously a method must be devised to define such a string sequence in the terminfo description, and at the same time allow terminfo to place any specified line and column in this sequence as required at runtime. Terminfo uses a system that is based on the printf(3) format conversion specification. The string is parsed and formatted into a sequence of characters which are then sent to the terminal to perform the desired operation.

A parameterized capability string can contain three types of object: ordinary characters which are just sent directly to the terminal; a conversion specification; and a parameter mechanism which uses a *push* and *pop* (Reverse Polish) stack system.

A conversion specification is triggered by the percent (%) character, in which following characters in the specification make up the instruction. For example, the sequence "%2d" means output a two-digit decimal number. A full list of the '%' encoded conversion specifications is given in Table 7.4.

Table 7.4

TERMINFO % ENCODED CONVERSION SPECIFICATIONS	
Sequence	*Description*
%c	Print pop() like %c in printf(3)
%%	Output the % character
%p[1-9]	Push() parameter 1 to 9
%P[a-z]	Variable a-z = pop()
%g[a-z]	Get and push() variable a-z
%'c'	Push() character constant c
%{nn}	Push() integer constant nn
%l	Pop() a string address and pop() its length
%[:[flags]][0-9[.0-9]][dsoxX]	Print pop() as in printf(3) flags are [-+#] and space. Leading + or - must be preceded by a colon (:)
%+ %- %* %/ %m	Arithmetic push(pop() op pop()) where op is the arithmetic operation. %m is modulus
%& %| %^	Bit push(pop() op pop()) where op is the bit operation
%= %> %< %A %O	Logical push(pop() op pop()) where op is the logical operation. %O is OR, %A is AND
%! %~	Unary push(pop() op pop()) where op is the unary operation as used in the C language
%i	For terminals that start numbering from 1 instead of 0 as with ANSI terminals. Add 1 to specified parameters
%?	"if" expression
%t	"then" expression
%e	"else" expression (optional)
%e%?	"else-if" expression (optional)
%;	"endif" expression

There are 8 registers in the stack system which can be programmed to handle both simple and complex operations as necessary. Normally you use it to *push* a parameter onto the stack before printing it in some way. For example, the definition for the aforementioned ansi cursor-addressing cup capability is cup=\E[%i%p1%d;%p2%dH. Figure 7.1 breaks down this sequence:

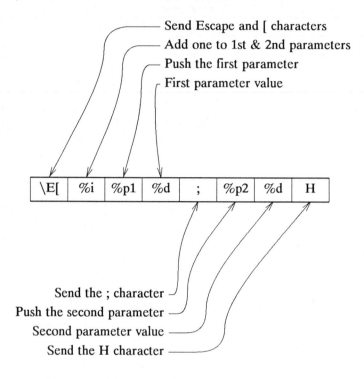

Figure 7.1: *Ansi cup sequence*

Note that the *%i* tells terminfo to add 1 to each parameter. This is necessary because ansi terminals start numbering cursor coordinates from 1 instead of 0 (zero). Since both *curses* and terminfo use zero-based cursor-addressing, both parameters must be incremented. To simplify, terminfo numbers an 80-column screen from 0 to 79, but the ansi terminal uses 1 to 80.

The example in Figure 7.2 is taken from a Hewlett Packard terminfo description. The same cursor-addressing capability (cup) is used but the string sequence is quite different. Note that this terminal requires the cursor coordinates to be specified as (column,line) rather than (line,column) so that the row and column are reversed. Also, a 6 millisecond padding is required after sending the sequence. The sequence in the terminfo description is cup=\E&a%p2%dc%p1%dY$<6>.

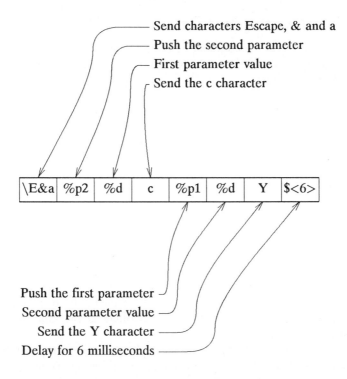

Figure 7.2: *Hewlett Packard cup sequence*

It is possible to do binary operations in a capability string. For example, we could define the ansi *cup* capability like this:

cup=\E[%p1%{1}%+%d;%p2%{1}%+%dH,

In effect, we have removed the *%i* from the definition and replaced it by telling terminfo to add 1 to each parameter using binary arithmetic. Binary arithmetic uses a postfix notation. That is, the operand is fixed to the end of the equation.

For example, if you want to add 1 to the first pushed parameter, the equation

push_value + 1

would be written like this:

push_value 1 +

and the string "%p1%{1}%+" does exactly that.

7.8 Conditional testing in strings

Terminfo also supports conditional testing within parameterized string capabilities. The system used is similar to that of programming in C (see Table 7.2). Generally the form is:

> if *expression*
> then
>   *statement A*
> else
>   *statement B*
> endif

Only one statement in the test is done. If the first *expression* is true then *statement A* is done, if not *statement B* is done. As soon as the condition is met were an expression is TRUE, no further testing is done. The *else* part of a test is optional, and *else-if* can also be used within a conditional test.

Conditional testing is mostly used to define the `sgr` string capability, when the terminal supports combined video attributes. That is, the terminal allows a character to be displayed with more than one attribute at the same time — for example, standout, blinking, and underlined.

`sgr` uses a 9-parameter string, with each parameter representing the condition of an attribute. That is, an attribute is either on (non-zero) or off (zero). The attributes are standout, underline, reverse, blink, dim, bold, invisible, protected, and alternate character set, and are specified in the `sgr` sequence in that order. In addition, not all attributes need to be supported. Only those that are tested for within `sgr` will be used.

As an example we will study the ansi `sgr` sequence:

> sgr = E[%?%p1%t7;%;%?%p2%t4;%;%?%p3%t7;%;
>   %?%p4%t5;%;%?%p6%t1;%;m,

Note that this line has been split into two so that it fits on the page. You would normally define this capability on one single line. This sometimes causes the screen to wrap while you are using the editor to create your description file.

Table 7.5 describes the sequences needed to turn on each video attribute on an ansi terminal. Note that each sequence described starts with the same escape string "\E[", and that they all end the same with the character "m".

Table 7.5

ANSI VIDEO ATTRIBUTES	
Attribute	*Escape sequence*
standout	\E[7;m
underline	\E[4;m
reverse	\E[7;m
blink	\E[5;m
dim	*not used*
bold	\E[1;m
invis	*not used*
protect	*not used*
alt char set	*not used*

To explain this further, the ansi sgr string sequence has been divided into its relevant conversion strings and the pseudo-code for each divisional part is given below.

\\E[	send sequence to initiate an escape sequence
%?%p1	if parameter 1 is true
%t	then
7;	send sequence to turn on *standout*.
%;	endif
%?%p2	if parameter 2 is true
%t	then
4;	send sequence to turn on *underline*.
%;	endif
%?%p3	if parameter 3 is true
%t	then
7;	send sequence to turn on *reverse*.
%;	endif
%?%p4	if parameter 4 is true
%t	then
5;	send sequence to turn on *blink*.
%;	endif

%?%p6	if parameter 6 is true
%t	then
1;	send sequence to turn on *bold*.
%;	endif
m	send final character that makes up the sequence.

Note that only the parameters for those attributes supported are given. The others are ignored since no test for them is defined.

It can be seen that a string capability can be defined by using a combination of sequences to generate a single sequence depending on a condition.

CHAPTER 8

Terminfo capabilities

This next chapter concentrates on *terminfo capabilities*. Each capability is briefly discussed and its use is explained.

The number of supported capabilities is growing with each new release of the UNIX System V operating system. Therefore it is possible that your system has even more capabilities than those covered here, which are supported on the UNIX system which I use: an AT&T UNIX System V.3 release 1 variant.

8.1 Introduction to the capabilities

When writing terminfo descriptions it is a good idea to familiarize yourself with all the supported capabilities of both your terminal and your UNIX system.

To help you build a terminfo description the capabilities have been split into ordered groups so that their explanation follows a logical reasoning. If you are building a terminfo description for the first time, you should read through each section carefully before you start. A list of cross-reference tables is provided in the Appendix. It is recommended that you refer to these while studying this chapter.

Capability definitions should be specified in the following order: boolean, numerics, and strings. Start with the basic capabilities and build your description logically. As you define a capability, test it before moving on to the next one — don't try and do it all at once. A good test is to get the UNIX editor *vi* to work in visual mode. For most UNIX installations this is all that is required, but sometimes it is necessary to introduce more advanced capabilities so that the terminal can be utilized fully by all *curses* and *terminfo* programs.

Before you attempt to write a new terminfo description, obtain a manufacturer's user manual for the terminal you are about to describe. Remember, test each capability before moving on to the next. Finally, if you do design a new terminal description, pass it on. You never know, someone may even improve it for you!

8.2 Setting up the terminal

You will need the terminal plugged in and set up ready for testing. Before you start, locate the terminal interface cable, and connect one end to an unused port on the back of the computer and the other to the back of the terminal. Note that not every computer has the same cable configuration. If the cable isn't configured to meet the terminals requirements, it may not work as expected or it may not work at all.

So that the terminal and the computer can communicate properly, make sure that the terminal is set up correctly. Some terminals have built-in firmware which you can use to set up such things as baud rate, X-on/X-off, parity, and so on. Consult the terminal's manual about how to do this.

You will also have to instantiate a **getty** on the port that you are using in order to logon to the UNIX system (see `inittab(4)` in the UNIX System V Programmer's Reference Manual and `getty(1M)` in the UNIX System V System Administrator's Reference Manual for more information on how to do this).

8.3 Boolean capabilities

By specifying a boolean capability within your description, you are setting a *flag*. This tells terminfo that the terminal can or can't use a capability depending on the capability's nature. Terminfo will then consider this information when manipulating the screen.

To specify a boolean capability, you merely include its definition in the terminfo description. No value needs to be assigned to it. The mere fact that it is specified tells terminfo that the particular flag is set.

8.4 Numeric capabilities

Numeric capabilities tell terminfo the physical size of an object according to the terminal described. You specify a *numeric* capability by assigning a numeric value to it. A special notation is used to differentiate between the assignment of string capabilities and numeric capabilities. For numeric capabilities you use the pound or hash character '#' for assignment. For example, to assign the value 24 to the numeric capability `lines` you would specify `lines#24` within the description.

8.5 String capabilities

String capabilities use the equals character '=' for assignment. For example, `"clear=E(^Z"` assigns the string sequence `"\E(^Z"` to the string capability `clear`.

Certain capabilities are used for input string sequences. These are sequences sent by the terminal in response to the user pressing a key which forms part of the keypad — such as function keys or arrow keys, for example. For example, the definition `"kf1=^Ac"` tells terminfo that if it receives the string sequence `"^Ac"`, it will recognize this as a key input from the function key labeled number one.

With the exception of capabilities used for input, you may specify padding in a string capability if it is necessary.

8.6 The basic capabilities

cols This definition tells terminfo how many columns (character positions) there are across the terminal screen. If your user manual does not specify this, enter a long line of characters until reaching the right edge of the screen and then simply count the characters.

lines This variable is used by terminfo to find out how many lines make up a full display on the terminal screen. Once again, if the user manual cannot help you, use the UNIX command **cat** to display a large text file on the screen, then just count how many lines make up the display area.

am If the terminal wraps around to the start of the next line when a line goes off the right edge of the screen, you should specify this boolean capability. You can test this by simply typing a long line until you reach the right edge of the screen. If the cursor does not wrap around when you reach the end of the line, don't specify am.

hc   This capability tells terminfo that the terminal is not a glass screen terminal but a hard-copy (paper-printing) terminal.

os   If the terminal overstrikes a character rather than clearing it first, then os should be defined (this applies only to hard-copy terminals). Overstriking causes both characters on the same character position to be displayed.

ul   If the terminal underlines characters by overstriking but leaves the character otherwise untouched, you should specify this boolean.

bw   If the terminal wraps around to the right-most edge of the screen on the previous line when you backspace from the left-most character position on the current line (column 0), specify this capability.

         It is important not to allow your programs to use this facility as terminfo may lose control of the terminal.

bel   This string capability is used to make the terminal sound a bell (normally Control-G).

cr   This string sequence is used to make the cursor move to the left-most position on the current line (carriage-return).

8.7 Local cursor manipulation

The following are all string sequences:

civis   Makes the cursor invisible.

cvvis   Makes the cursor brighter than normal.

cnorm   Undoes the effect of civis and cvvis and makes the cursor appear normal.

cub1   Moves the cursor to the previous character position on the current line.

cuf1   Makes the cursor move right to the next character position on the current line. This a non-destructive move. In other words, characters are not erased when the cursor is moved.

cud1   Makes the cursor move down to the line below the current one. The cursor should remain in the current column position. Note that on most terminals it is impossible to write in the bottom right-hand corner of the screen. If the current column is the last one on the line and the line below is the last line, most terminals automatically scroll up if the cursor is forced to move into this position. For this reason, *curses* never writes in this position of the screen unless scrolling is imminent.

cuu1   Makes the cursor move up to the previous line. The cursor should remain in the current column.

home   Makes the cursor move to the upper left-hand corner of the screen (home position). Terminfo will use this capability if *cup* (see Section 8.9) is not defined.

hd   Makes the cursor move down by half a normal line space. This is normally a feature of hard-copy terminals although there are a few glass screen terminals that also support it.

hu   Makes the cursor move up by half a normal line space (see hu above).

nel   This sequence (usually \r followed by \n) should be given if the terminal has a sequence to move the cursor to the beginning of the next line.

8.8 Tabs and tabstops

xt   If the terminal destructively overwrites characters with spaces when a tab is used, you should specify this boolean capability. You can test this on the command line. First use the **stty** command to turn off erase character echoing. Issue the command **stty -echoe**. Enter a string of garbage characters, then backspace over them. If you then enter a tab and the characters are overwritten, specify this flag. Don't forget to reset the terminal driver. To do this, issue the command **stty echoe**.

it   If the terminal has hardware tabstops set when it is powered up, you should assign to this numeric capability the number of character positions which tabs are initially set to.

cbt   If the terminal supports hardware tabstops, then this string sequence makes the cursor move backwards to the previous tabstop position (backtab).

ht   If the terminal supports hardware tabs, this string sequence advances the cursor to the next tabstop position (normally Control-I).

tbc   If there is a sequence to clear all tabstops, then you should specify this with tbc.

hts   If there is a sequence to set tabstops in the current column of every line, you should specify this with hts.

8.9 Absolute cursor addressing

cup   This string sequence moves the cursor non-destructively to any given line and column on the screen. It uses a parameterized string (see Section 7.7); the first encoded parameter specifies the line address, and the second specifies the column address. This is a very important capability, so make sure you test it fully.

smcup   If the terminal is required to be set into a special mode before using cursor addressing (cup), then the sequence for initializing this mode can be given.

rmcup   Similar to smcup, this string sequence is used to end *cursor-addressing* mode.

nrrmc   You should specify this boolean if the capability smcup cannot reverse the effect of rmcup.

The following are parameterized strings:

cub   Contains the sequence to move the cursor to the left a given number of places.

cuf   Contains the sequence to move the cursor to the right a given number of places.

cuu   Contains the sequence to move the cursor up a given number of lines.

cud   Contains the sequence to move the cursor down a given number of lines.

hpa   Contains the sequence to move the cursor to a given column address on the current line.

vpa   Contains the sequence to move the cursor to a given line address on the screen. The column address remains the same.

ll   If the terminal has a sequence to move the cursor to the lower left corner of the display area, this should be given in ll. This is normally used only if cup is not defined.

8.10 Display erasure

clear   This string sequence is used to erase the entire screen. After the screen is cleared, the cursor is moved into the top left-hand corner of the screen (home position).

ed   This string sequence erases from the current cursor position to the end of the display area without moving the cursor from its current position.

el   This string sequence erases from the current cursor position to the end of the current line without moving the cursor from its current position.

el1   This string sequence erases from the beginning of the current line through the current cursor position without moving the cursor from its current position.

8.11 Line editing

il1   If the terminal can insert a blank line above the current one and leave
          the cursor at the beginning of that new line, you should specify this
          string sequence with this capability.

il   If the terminal can insert a given number of blank lines above the
          current one and leave the cursor at the beginning of the previous new
          line, you should specify this parameterized string sequence with this
          capability.

dl1   If the terminal can delete the current line and all the lines below the
          deleted line are shifted up, you should specify this parameterized string
          sequence with this capability.

dl   If the terminal can delete a given number of lines including the current
          line, and all lines below the deleted lines are shifted up to the current
          line, you should specify this string sequence with this capability.

8.12 Insert/delete modes

smir   If the terminal requires a special character sequence to enter *insert*
          mode, then give this sequence with smir.

rmir   If the terminal requires a special character sequence to exit *insert* mode,
          then give this sequence with rmir.

smdc   If the terminal requires a special character sequence to enter *delete*
          mode, then give this sequence with smdc.

rmdc   If the terminal requires a special character sequence to exit *delete* mode,
          then give this sequence with rmdc.

in   If the terminal uses a NULL to insert white space on the screen instead
          of the space character, specify this boolean capability. On some
          terminals a NULL (actually octal 200) is used instead of a space to get a
          blank on the screen. If the terminal can distinguish between the two, it
          will delete the NULL when you insert a character over it, whereas a
          blank character will be shifted right.
              Note that the NULL character '\0' placed in a string will cause all
          characters after it including the NULL to be ignored, therefore it is not
          possible to place a NULL character within a string capability and hope
          that it will be sent to the terminal (or printer). Sending the octal value
          '\200' where a NULL is needed may not work either, since not all
          terminals ignore the eighth bit. Devices that adhere completely to the

standard ASCII character set (that is, they use all eight bits) will treat '\0' and '\200' as two different characters.

mir   If the terminal allows the cursor to be moved while in *insert* mode, then this capability should be defined. Before specifying this capability, make sure the terminal interprets the cup capability properly.

ich1   If the terminal requires a special character sequence to be sent before a character can be inserted into the current position on the current line, it should be specified in this capability. All other characters on the line after the inserted character should shift right, and the last position is possibly lost.

If the terminal can enter *insert* mode via smir, you should specify that instead, unless the owner's manual specifies that both sequences are required, in which case specify this capability anyway. At least one method is required.

ich   Some terminals support a special sequence that allows a number of given characters to be inserted at once. This is similar to ich1 but more economical since this sequence can be just sent once before sending a given number of characters. ich1, on the other hand, must be sent before each character to be inserted.

ich will be used by terminfo instead of ich1 wherever possible if it has been defined. It requires one parameter.

dch1   Similar to ich1, this sequence is used for entering *delete* mode before deleting a character. If the terminal requires it, specify the sequence with dch1. All characters after the deleted character on the current line are shifted left.

dch   Similar to ich, this sequence requires one parameter and is used for entering *delete* mode before deleting a number of given characters.

ech   If the terminal supports the capability to erase a given number of characters without moving the cursor, it should be given in ech which requires one parameter.

8.13 Delays and padding

npc   If the terminal does not have a pad character, then define this boolean capability.

ip   If the terminal requires padding before inserting a character when in *insert* mode, then specify the number of milliseconds required with this string capability (see Section 7.6).

Note that padding is primarily used by hard-copy terminals. Padding specified in the capabilities cr, ind, cub1, ff and tab can be used to set the necessary delay bits within the *tty* driver.

rmp   If the terminal requires padding during character transmission while not in *insert* mode, then specify the number of milliseconds required with this string capability.

pad   If the terminal uses a character other than NULL (zero) for a pad character, then specify this character with pad. Note that only the first character of this string capability is used.

pb   This capability is essentially only of use to hard-copy terminals. Certain capabilities control padding in the *tty* driver (see Section 2.1) to instantiate a delay (see Section 7.6). Such capabilities can ignore this delay time below baud rates specified in this numeric capability.

8.14 Paged memory terminals

da   If the terminal can retain screen information in a page of memory above the display page, then define this boolean capability.

       Some terminals have local memory which is addressable. This memory normally sits above and/or below the normal screen display. If the terminal does support this feature, then terminfo must be informed so that it can handle scrolling properly. For example, when the screen is scrolled forward, blank lines may come up from the bottom page.

       If the terminal has only memory-relative addressing and no screen-relative addressing, then you will have to find a way to set up one screen-sized window within the terminal's local memory to make cursor addressing work properly (see mrcup below).

db   Like da, the terminal can retain screen information in a page of memory below the display page.

mrcup If the terminal uses memory-related cursor addressing, then specify the sequence to address the cursor with this capability (see also cup).

lm   If the terminal has more lines in memory than specified by lines, then you should specify how many lines of memory the terminal has by assigning the number of lines to this numeric capability. Specifying lm#0 tells terminfo that the number of lines making up the screen is not fixed, and that memory exists for more lines than the screen can accommodate.

8.15 Alternate character set mode

smacs If the terminal supports an alternate character set, then the sequence to enter alternate-character-set mode can be given in this capability string. Note that no provision is given for more than one alternate character set.

rmacs   Similar to smacs, this sequence is used to exit *alternate-character-set*
         mode.

Table 8.1

ALTERNATE CHARACTER SET		
Default	*Line drawing character code*	*Description*
+	l	upper left corner
+	m	lower left corner
+	k	upper right corner
+	j	lower right corner
+	u	right tee (⊣)
+	t	left tee (⊢)
+	v	bottom tee (⊥)
+	w	top tee (⊤)
-	q	horizontal line
|	x	vertical line
+	n	plus
-	o	scan line 1
_	s	scan line 9
+	,	diamond
:	a	checker board (stipple)
,	f	degree symbol
#	g	plus/minus
<	,	arrow pointing left
>	+	arrow pointing right
v	.	arrow pointing down
^	-	arrow pointing up
#	h	board of squares
#	I	lantern symbol
#	0	solid square block
~	o	bullet

acsc   This string contains a set of two-character codes. The first character is
        the line-drawing character code (see Table 8.1). The second is the
        character the terminal uses to print the glyph, when set in *alternate-
        character-set* mode (see also Section 5.3). The code system is based on
        the *DEC VT100* and *AT&T Teletype 5420* alternate character set codes

(see Tables 5.1 and 8.1). For example, if your terminal uses the character 'V' for a *lower-left-corner* glyph, and the character 'Z' for a *lower-right-corner* glyph, your acsc string would look like "acsc=mVjZ".

If *alternate-character-set* mode is set and an alternate character code is not defined in the acsc string specification, a character from the default alternate character set is used.

enacs   If the terminal supports an alternate character set and requires a command sequence to be sent before entering *alternate-character-set* mode, give this string sequence in enacs.

8.16 Scrolling

csr   Normally when the terminal scrolls, the top line is lost and all other lines on the screen are shifted up one; a blank line is then attached to the bottom of the screen. Some terminals, however, have a modifiable scrolling region which can be set so that only those lines within the scrolling area are scrolled.

This string sequence applies to those terminals which have modifiable scrolling regions only (notably the **DEC VT100**). This string is a parameterized sequence where the first parameter will be replaced with the line number for the new top line of the scrolling region, and the second parameter will be replaced with the line number for the new bottom line of the scrolling region.

wind   Some terminals can set up a window on the terminal for a scrolling area which is not limited to the width of the screen. For such terminals, this 4-parameter string capability is given. The first two parameters specify the new top and bottom scrolling region, the second two parameters specify the left-most and right-most columns of the window which will be affected.

ind   This string sequence is used to scroll the entire screen up a line. To do this you move to the bottom left-hand corner of the screen, then issue the ind (index) sequence.

ri   This string sequence is used to scroll the entire screen down a line. To do this you move to the top left-hand corner of the screen, then issue the ri (reverse index) sequence.

indn   If the terminal has a sequence for scrolling up a given number of lines, then it should be given with this parameterized capability.

rin   As with indn, if the terminal has a sequence for scrolling down a given number of lines, then it should be given with this parameterized capability.

Note that capabilities ind, ri, indn and rin may cause terminfo to lose control of the screen if they are not used at their appropriate edge of the screen.

8.17 Soft labels

lh   If the terminal supports soft labels, you should specify how many lines the soft-label line occupies on the screen with this numeric capability.

lw   Like lh, this numeric capability is assigned the width in character positions of the soft labels.

nlab   This numeric capability should be given the number of soft labels supported by the terminal.

pln   If the terminal supports programmable soft labels, specify the string sequence to program them with this parameterized capability. The first parameter specifies the label number to program, the second is the string to place in the label.

rmln   If the terminal has a sequence to turn off the soft labels, then give that sequence with rmln.

smln   If the terminal has a sequence to turn on soft labels, then give that sequence with smln.

lf*n*   The capabilities lf0 – lf10 can be used to specify a name other than the default name given to a function key if it is not the same. Only the first 11 function keys can be renamed. For example, the internal default name for function key 5 is "f5"; if this differs from the label on the keyboard, then you can give its preferred name with the capability lf5.
        Note that, although the function key labels can be renamed, no function currently exists within terminfo which uses this facility (UNIX System V.3).

8.18 Highlighting and other attributes

chts   If the cursor is hard to see — for example, if it is a non-blinking underline — specifying this flag tells terminfo to try to make it more visible: for example, a reverse video block. (See also cvvis.)

blink   If the terminal has a *blink* mode, give the string sequence to turn this mode on. Characters displayed in this mode will blink on the screen (on some terminals the entire screen blinks).

bold   This string sequence is used to turn on *bold* mode. Characters displayed in this mode will be highlighted bold or extra bright.

dim   This string sequence is used to turn on *dim* mode. Characters displayed in this mode will be displayed dimmer than usual.

invis   This string sequence is used to turn on *invisible* mode. Characters displayed in this mode will be blank or invisible.

rev   This string sequence is used to turn on *reverse-video* mode. Characters are normally displayed white on a black background. However, characters displayed in this mode will be in reverse video, that is, black on a white background.

sgr0   If any attributes are set, then this string is used to turn them off so that normal character output occurs.

smso   This string sequence is used to turn on *standout* mode. Characters displayed in this mode use the terminal's best highlighting mode, which is normally reverse video.

      This mode is typically used by *curses*-driven programs to display error messages and so on. Whichever mode you choose for standout, it should cause characters to be displayed so that they differ visibly from others on the screen.

rmso   This string sequence is used to turn off *standout* mode.

xmc   If by entering or exiting *standout* mode causes one or more blank spaces to appear on the screen, you should assign to this numeric capability the number of spaces that are displayed.

msgr   If the terminal allows the cursor to be moved while in *standout* mode, specify this boolean capability. This means that cursor motion can be done without leaving traces of standout wherever the cursor has been.

smul   This string sequence is used to turn on *underline* mode. Characters displayed in this mode will be underlined.

rmul   This string sequence is used to turn off *underline* mode.

uc   If the terminal has a string sequence which can underline the current character, then shift to the next column position. You should give this in uc.

flash   Specify this sequence if the terminal can flash the entire screen. The cursor must not be moved during the flash. This sequence is useful for indicating an error condition instead of using bel. If the terminal can't flash, it is best to assign the same sequence as defined for bel rather than leave it undefined.

sgr   If the terminal supports combined attributes which can be set by choice, they should be encoded in this parameterized string (see Section 7.8). This string uses 9 parameters which specify the condition of each attribute. That is, it is either on (non-zero) or off (zero).

prot   If the terminal has a *protect* mode, then define this sequence to turn it on. When in *protect* mode, characters sent to the terminal are protected from accidental erasure, and each character sent contains a write-protect attribute. The cursor cannot re-enter this character position but instead passes over it. Note that screen scrolling does not usually work while characters exist on the screen in this mode.

8.19 Function and other special keys

kf*n*   There may be several function keys on the keyboard. Each function key supported sends a unique string sequence which you can define in these capabilities. Note: *n* corresponds to the function key number as shown on the keyboard. You should define only those keys which are supported by the terminal.

To find out the string sequence sent by any function or cursor keys, use the UNIX command **cat -v**. Press each key followed by the return key, and the sequence sent will then be displayed. Note, if **cat -v** displays "^[" as part of any sequence this normally implies the escape character, any other character preceded by '^' implies a control character. So the sequence ^[A translates to "Escape followed by the character A", and the sequence ^A translates to "Control-A".

k*xxx*   If any special keys are labeled other than function keys or the normal character keys (such as arrow and cursor keys, or keys marked page-up etc.), their string sequences should be described using their relevant terminfo capabilities. The cross-reference tables in the Appendix detail those keys supported by terminfo and what their *capname* labels are (they are self-explanatory).

pfkey   If the terminal supports programmable function keys, then this parameterized string specifies the sequence to send. The first parameter is the function key to program (only the first 10 function keys are currently supported); the second is the string that is sent by the function key when it is pressed.

Note that programming function keys may make the terminal send sequences which differ from those defined in the original terminfo description.

pfloc   This sequence is similar to pfkey except that the string programmed is executed only in *local* mode by the terminal.

pfx   This is similar to pfkey. If the terminal supports programmable function keys, you program them using the same method as with pfkey using this parameterized string sequence. The terminal sets up its

keyboard functions keys to output the string sequence that you specified
— for example, this could be a UNIX command, like **ls -al**. The
specified string is transmitted to the computer when the programmed
function key is pressed.

smkx   Give this sequence if the terminal has a sequence to enable the keypad,
that is, keys other than the normal character keys. If function keys
and/or other special keys are to be used within a *curses* program, then
curses must be able to enable *keypad* mode.

rmkx   Give this sequence if the terminal has a sequence to disable the keypad.

8.20 Extra status line terminals

hs   If the terminal has an extra line (status line) at the bottom of the screen
which can be accessed via the normal cursor-addressing method, then
this boolean capability should be defined.

wsl   Normally the *status line* has the same number of columns as other lines
across the screen, but if it does not, use this numeric capability to specify
its width. If this capability is not specified, terminfo assumes the value
of cols for all lines including the status line.

dsl   If the terminal can turn off the status line or erase its contents, do this
with dsl.

tsl   Define this string capability if the terminal has a sequence to move to a
given column in the status line. The parameter specifies the column
address within the status line.

fsl   This sequence, to be used in conjunction with tsl, returns the cursor
from the status line and moves it to where it was before the tsl
sequence was issued.

8.21 Initialization

is2   Essentially, the sequences for initializing the terminal are sent by the
UNIX command **tput**. The command **tput init** should be issued before
any program that uses terminfo (including *curses*). Ideally, this
command should be run from your **.profile** at login time.
  The purpose of these initialization strings is to set up the terminal so
that it is ready for use with *curses* or terminfo-based programs. Once
transmitted to the terminal, they should place it into its relevant
operating modes, which are consistent with the rest of the terminal's
terminfo description. Generally, is2 is the most common string used
for initializing the terminal. The command **tput init** does the following:

(1)   If the capability `iprog` is defined (which should contain the full path name of a UNIX command), then the program specified in this string is executed. This may be a special case program which initializes the terminal in a way that terminfo can't. Although this facility exists, there are currently no terminals in the terminfo database that use it.

(2)   If `is1` is defined, this is sent to the terminal followed by `is2`.

(3)   Tabstops are initialized using `tbc` and `hts`.

(4)   If `if` is defined, the contents of this file are sent to the terminal.

(5)   Finally, the sequence for `is3` is sent, if it is defined.

if   If the terminal initialization sequence is too long to fit in the description file, it should be put in a file which will be printed (sent) to the terminal. Thus, this string capability contains the full path-name of a UNIX file. It is normal for terminals that use this method to store their initialization files in the */usr/lib/tabset* directory.

iprog   This string sequence contains the full path-name of a UNIX executable which is used to initialize the terminal (see above).

is1   This string contains the primary initialization sequence (see above) which may be used in special cases.

is3   This string contains the final initialization sequence (see above) which may be used in special cases.

mgc   This sequence clears both left and right soft margins.
          At the time of writing, there are no functions within the terminfo library which use `mgc`, `smgl` or `smgr`. Also, within the terminfo database the only terminal descriptions which define them are for AT&T manufactured terminals.

smgl   This sequence is used to clear the left soft margin.

smgr   This sequence is used to clear the right soft margin.

8.22 Resetting the terminal

rs2   As with the initialization capabilities, these strings are usually used to reset the terminal to a *sane* operating mode if it gets into an unusable state. This often happens if a *curses* program exits abnormally without calling `endwin()`.
          Normally, these strings are sent to the terminal by the UNIX command **tput reset**, which leaves the terminal in a completely *sane* mode. The command **tput reset** does essentially the same as **tput init**

except that the rs1, rs2 and rs3 strings are also sent.

rf   If the terminal's reset string is too long to fit in the description file, then rf should define the full path-name of a UNIX file (normally in /usr/lib/tabset) which will be printed to the terminal.

rs1   This string contains the primary reset sequence (see above) which may be used in special cases.

rs3   This string contains the secondary reset sequence (see above) which may be used in special cases.

8.23 Saving and restoring the cursor

sc   Use this if the terminal has a sequence for saving the current cursor position locally.

rc   This sequence restores the cursor to the position last saved with sc.

8.24 Auxiliary printer control

These string capabilities are provided for the control of an auxiliary printer connected *locally* to the terminal.

mc0   If it is possible to print the contents of the display area, give this sequence with mc0.

mc4   This string turns off the auxiliary printer port.

mc5   This string turns on the auxiliary printer port.

mc5p   Use this if the terminal has a sequence which will print out a given number of bytes from the display area. This string takes a single parameter specifying the number of bytes to print (which must not exceed 255).

mc5i   Give this boolean if the terminal has an auxiliary printer port which, when activated, stops output to the display screen, but instead sends output directly to the printer port.

8.25 Similar terminals

use   If the terminal you are describing is similar to another which has already been described you can tell terminfo to use that description by using this capability (see Section 7.2).

8.26 Miscellaneous capabilities

rep   If the terminal has a special sequence for character repetition, then specify this with rep. This saves transmission time if several identical characters are to be sent. Two parameters are used: the first is the character to be repeated, and the second specifies how many times to repeat it.

eo   Some terminals can overstrike a character with another and leave both characters showing. Specifying this boolean capability tells terminfo that the space character erases all the data in the character at the current cursor position (see also os).

eslok Specify this capability if the terminal has an extra line (often called the *status line*) and the escape-character (or keys that send sequences containing the escape-character) works while the cursor is in it (function keys for example).

gn   If the terminal you are describing is not a known terminal type such as a *dialup*, you should specify this capability so that terminfo can complain that it doesn't know how to communicate with it.

hz   If the terminal cannot display the tilde '~' character, this boolean should be specified (*Vi* will use the '^' character instead).

km   If the terminal has a special key which sets *8-bit transmission* mode, this boolean should be specified; it is usually sent by a key such as *Alt* or *meta*.

smm   Use this if the terminal has a sequence to turn on *8-bit transmission* mode (*meta* mode). Characters sent in this mode are sent with parity; that is, all 8 bits are sent. Terminfo normally defaults to *7-bit transmission* mode.

rmm   This sequence is used to turn off *8-bit transmission* mode.

xon   If the terminal uses X-on/X-off handshaking flow control, you should specify this boolean capability.

smxon If the terminal can toggle X-on/X-off handshaking using string sequences, give the sequence for turning on this mode. Note that you should also define xon.

rmxon As with smxon, this turns off X-on/X-off handshaking.

xoffc If the terminal uses characters other than ^S/^Q (Control-S/Control-Q) for handshaking control. The X-off character is given with xoffc.

xonc   The X-on character is given with xonc (see above).

ff   This string sequence is used for hard-copy terminals and is used to send a form-feed or page-eject sequence which may require padding (see also **pad**).

xhp   If the erase to end-of-line capability (el) must be used to remove characters displayed in standout, then define this capability.

xsb   This is primarily provided for Beehive Superbee terminals which cannot transmit the escape character or Control-C. Instead, function-key-1 is used for escape, and function-key-2 for Control-C. Specify this boolean if this reflects your terminal.

smam   If the terminal has a sequence to turn on automatic margins (am), this should be given with **smam**.

rmam   If the terminal has a sequence to turn off automatic margins, this should be given with **rmam**.

xenl   Give this boolean if the terminal ignores a line-feed after an automatic margin wrap (am).

CHAPTER 9

The low-level terminfo library

This next chapter discusses the low-level terminfo library routines and termcap emulation facilities. *Curses* is, in fact, a platform of routines built on top of terminfo. It is recommended that you use *curses* if you want to build a program that drives the terminal screen in a hardware-independent way.

However, sometimes it is necessary to write programs which need to access the terminfo database for reasons other than manipulating the screen. For example, **tput**, **infocmp** and **tic** are among a few of the UNIX commands which query the terminfo database and do not necessarily manipulate the screen. Therefore these low-level functions are also described.

In this chapter you will learn how to access the terminfo database directly. Terminfo has evolved just as UNIX System V has, and many new capabilities have been added to the database since it was introduced. For this reason, terminfo implementations tend to vary, mainly due to improved functionality. However, the routines discussed within this chapter are those which are supported on most implementations of UNIX System V.

9.1 Introduction

The *low-level* terminfo routines are provided for the following:

- Programmers who need to manipulate the terminal screen directly without using the *curses* library. For example, you may want to create your own kind of *curses* library.

- Programmers who need to use the terminfo database facilities, to reprogram function keys, for example.

- Programmers who need to query the terminfo database. For example, the UNIX program **infocmp** does this.

Under UNIX System V the terminfo library comes packaged as part of the *curses* library. Therefore, to compile a program which makes use of the terminfo routines, use the command line syntax the same way as for compiling a *curses* program. (For more details on how to compile a terminfo program see Section 2.10.)

The process of manipulating a terminal in an independent way must be adhered to at all times when designing a program which uses these routines. Supposing that you want to move the cursor to a new position on the screen — there are a number of things to consider: does the terminal support absolute cursor-addressing (cup)? Can it be moved while in *standout* mode (msgr)? Should the terminal be in a special mode before using these capabilities (e.g. smcup, rmcup)? and so on.

The designers of *curses* have learned much about such quirks during its evolution, and have considered such idioms during the creation of the *curses* package. Be aware that using the terminfo library directly may render your program unusable (in effect, hardware-dependent) on certain terminals. If you want to manipulate the terminal screen it is recommended that you use *curses* and not terminfo.

While writing terminfo-based programs it is strongly recommended that you familiarize yourself with the facilities provided by both the terminfo database and the terminfo library. The Appendix contains cross-reference tables which will be invaluable to you during the course of design.

9.2 Setting things up

There are two header files which must be included in your terminfo program. They are <curses.h> and <term.h>, in that order. These files import the necessary definitions for each capability supported by your terminfo package into your C program. They also include various variables, structures and arrays which will be used throughout your program design.

You start a terminfo program with the following function:

```
setupterm(term, fildes, errret);
```

This function reads in the necessary information about the terminal from the terminfo database and initializes the aforementioned variables, structures and so on. To figure out the dimensions of the terminal screen, this function looks for the environment variables LINES and/or COLUMNS. If they exist these values will be used for the terminal's dimensions instead of the values specified in the terminfo description lines and cols.

setupterm() returns an integer. Its arguments, in order, specify: the name of the terminal, an open file descriptor for output, and a pointer to an integer variable used to store a value if an error occurs — you are responsible for defining its space.

Incidentally, the *curses* start-up function initscr() indirectly calls setupterm() as part of the *curses* initialization sequence. Like *curses*, terminfo must also know what type of terminal it is working with, and this function is used primarily for this purpose. The argument term is typically a NULL pointer, which instructs terminfo to use getenv("TERM") to obtain the current terminal type. But you could use it to specify a terminal name explicitly.

The argument fildes is not a stdio file pointer, it is a UNIX file descriptor. It is an open file handle to which all output is to be sent and where all internal ioctl() is done (the standard output, which is normally 1). Using this file handle setupterm() checks the *tty* driver mode bits modifying those which may prevent the correct operation of the other low-level terminfo routines. If setupterm() finds that tabs are being expanded to spaces by the *tty* driver, then this mode is turned off, because the tab character is used by some terminals for different functions. For example, some terminals use it to move right 1 space whereas others use it to move the cursor right 8 spaces. Even if setupterm() knows which method was used, you might not have set up the hardware tabs correctly. So, if terminfo finds that the system is expanding tabs it will disable both tab and backtab in the tty driver.

setupterm() also provides comprehensive error handling features. If errret is a NULL pointer, terminfo will handle errors automatically — it will print an error message to the screen and then exit the program. Thus, you would normally just issue the call:

```
setupterm((char *)0, 1, (int *)0);
```

without testing for an error condition. You can arrange setupterm() so that you can handle errors yourself. If errret is not NULL, this function will return OK or ERR depending on the condition. At the same time it will store the status value in errret which specifies the return condition. The following code example makes this evident:

```
#include <curses.h>
#include <term.h>

main(argc,argv)
int argc;
char *argv[];
{
    char *term_name;
    char *getenv();
    int errret;

    switch(argc) {
      case 1:
        if((term_name = getenv("TERM")) == (char *)NULL) {
            fprintf(stderr,"TERM not set\n");
            exit(1);
        }
        break;
      case 2:
        term_name = argv[1];
        break;
      default:
        fprintf(stderr,"Usage: %s [ terminal-name ]\n",argv[0]);
        exit(1);
    }

    if(setupterm(term_name, 1, &errret) == ERR) {
        if(errret == 0)
            fprintf(stderr,"Can't find terminfo entry\n");
        else if(errret == -1)
            fprintf(stderr,"Can't find terminfo database\n");
        exit(1);
    }
/* processing is continued here */
}
```

In this example we let the user decide which terminal to use. If the user supplies
the argument argv[1], then this is assumed to be the name of the terminal to
use throughout the program. However, if no argument is given (argc == 1),
then the default terminal is used, which is presumably defined in the environment
variable TERM. Beware of TERM — you should *always* check that this is set in the
environment. You can do this with getenv("TERM"). If the user does not set
TERM then setupterm() will use the terminal type "unknown". This method is
commonly used by programs such as **infocmp** which allow you to specify the

name of the terminal to use on the command line. Also, the address of `errret` is passed instead of a NULL pointer. `setupterm()` will use this area to place status information which we then go on to test. If the status value returned is 0 (zero), then the terminfo description for the terminal used was not found and a message to that effect is printed. Similarly, if the value is -1, then the terminfo database could not be found.

9.3 Changing the terminal type

As we discovered earlier, `setupterm()` initializes a number of variables and structures which make up the terminfo environment. Part of this initialization includes setting up an internal structure containing all the terminal's capabilities: boolean, numeric and strings. This structure is of type `TERMINAL`, and a pointer `cur_term` is provided which initially points to one of these `TERMINAL` structures containing all this information. The space for the structure which `cur_term` points to is allocated internally by `setupterm()`, and it is not static. This means that every time `setupterm()` is called it reserves space for a new `TERMINAL` structure which `cur_term` then points to.   `setupterm()` fills this new structure with the information obtained from the specified terminal's terminfo description instead of reusing the same previously allocated space. Therefore, we are able to retain the capability information of each terminal for which `setupterm()` was called on by keeping a copy of the `cur_term` pointer each time `setupterm()` is called. We can use this to manipulate more than one terminal.

The following example sends the `clear_screen` sequence to two terminal screens. The controlling terminal is the one the program was executed from and uses the default **$TERM** for its terminal type. The other terminal type is specified on the command line together with its UNIX device file name. In this example, the program is set up so that it will send the correct capability sequences to both terminal screens even though they may be different terminal types. Ideally, we want to organize the space for both `TERMINAL` structures when we start the program, then swap between them as required. The terminfo function `set_curterm(nterm)` allows us to do this. `nterm` is a pointer to a `TERMINAL` structure which is assumed to have already been filled in by `setupterm()`.

```
#include <curses.h>
#include <term.h>
#include <fcntl.h>

int current_fd;

main(argc,argv)
int argc;
char *argv[];
```

```
{
    TERMINAL *terminal1;
    TERMINAL *terminal2;
    int putterm();
    int fd;

    if(argc != 3) {
        fprintf(stderr,"Usage: %s device TERM\n",argv[0]);
        exit(1);
    }

    if((fd = open(argv[1],O_WRONLY)) < 0) {
        perror(argv[1]);
        exit(1);
    }

    setupterm((char *)0,1,(int *)0);
    terminal1 = cur_term;

    setupterm(argv[2],fd,(int *)0);
    terminal2 = cur_term;

    current_fd = 1;
    set_curterm(terminal1);
    tputs(clear_screen, 1, putterm);

    current_fd = fd;
    set_curterm(terminal2);
    tputs(clear_screen, 1, putterm);

}

putterm(c)
int c;
{
    write(current_fd,&c,1);
}
```

After validating the command line argument list, an attempt to open the
specified device for writing is made. The file descriptor returned from open() is
later used to send output to the other terminal. setupterm() is called once for
each terminal, and each time a copy of the cur_term pointer is saved. A global
variable current_fd is then initialized. This variable is used by the putterm()

function which outputs characters via `tputs()`. In a moment we will learn what `tputs()` is used for, but for now it is the terminfo function which actually sends the *clear-screen* sequence to each terminal. The function `set_curterm()` resets the terminfo environment so that all the internal variables reflect the terminal we want to deal with. After calling `set_curterm()`, the `cur_term` pointer points to the desired `TERMINAL` structure containing its terminal capabilities. `tputs()` then uses this information to send the correct sequence. This is done for both terminals.

If at any time you want to free up the space allocated for a `TERMINAL` structure you can use the function `del_curterm(oldterm)`. The argument `oldterm` must point to a valid `TERMINAL` structure for which space has been previously allocated by `setupterm()`. This function frees up all the memory associated with the `TERMINAL` structure and makes it available for further use. Be aware, though, that if you pass `del_curterm()` a pointer to the controlling terminal environment, you must call `setupterm()` again before referring to its capability information. If you do not, you may be referring to illegal memory locations which will make the program dump core.

Incidentally, `setupterm()` also initializes the global variable `ttytype`. This is an array of characters containing the list of names for the terminal which was found at the beginning of the terminfo description. Other available character string arrays are:

```
char *boolnames[], *boolcodes[], *boolfnames[];
char *numnames[], *numcodes[], *numfnames[];
char *strnames[], *strcodes[], *strfnames[];
```

These names, codes and fnames are: *capnames* as used for defining terminfo descriptions; *termcap* codes for use with the termcap emulation routines; and *C-language variables* used in the terminfo low-level routines. These are listed in the Appendix.

9.4 Outputting the capabilities

The process of sending a capability string sequence to the terminal is usually done with the function `tputs()`:

```
tputs(terminfo_string, affected_line_count, putc_function)
```

`tputs()` takes the `terminfo_string` and applies padding to it. The third argument to `tputs()` is the address of a function which you must supply. `tputs()` then uses this function to pass the string one character at a time. This output function can be any function which takes a single character argument and can output it to the terminal in some way. Normally you would use a function which simply calls `putchar()` from the `stdio` package. In fact, terminfo

conveniently provides the function putp(str), which does this for you. putp()
uses putchar() indirectly to call tputs() with tputs(str,1,putchar). You
can't use putchar() itself because it is a macro defined in <stdio.h> and you
can't pass the address of a macro to a function, but you can create a function
which uses it and pass the address of that instead. In the previous example
program which clears the screen on two terminals, we provide the output
function putterm() for this, which simply writes a single character to the
terminal associated with the file descriptor, current_fd. putterm() simply
uses the UNIX system call write() to output the character.

The affected_line_count is the number of lines which padding is applied
to, but padding will only be applied if it is specified in the string capability to
send. In other words, unless padding is specified within the capability string in
the terminal's terminfo description, it won't be applied. If it is specified then the
affected delay time of the padding applied is multiplied by the number specified
in the argument: affected_line_count. It is evident that a value of 1 for
affected_line_count has no effect on the delay time specified in the
description. Consequently, it is also possible to tell terminfo to ignore padding,
even though it may be specified in the string, by setting affected_line_count
to 0 (zero).

The string which you pass tputs() or putp() must be a terminfo-defined C
variable. These variables are #defined in <term.h> and have symbolic names
for convenience (see Appendix). The following function uses several of these
variables to create a clear-screen function:

```
clearscreen()
{
    int x;
    char *tparm();
    int my_putchar();

    if(clear_screen)
        putp(clear_screen);
    else if(cursor_home && clr_eos) {
        putp(cursor_home);
        putp(clr_eos);
    } else if(clr_eos && cursor_address) {
        tputs(tparm(cursor_address,0,0),1,my_putchar);
        putp(clr_eos);
    } else {
        for(x = 0;x <= lines; x++)
            printf("\r\n");
        fflush(stdout);
    }
}
```

```
my_putchar(c)
int c;
{
    putchar(c);
}
```

This function will clear the screen one way or another.

When `tputs()` is called it is passed the address of our function `my_putchar()`. Note that since it is known to be a function (because we defined it that way), the C language '&' operator is not necessary; the compiler will arrange for the address to be passed.

We have also introduced another terminfo function `tparm()`. This function takes up to 10 arguments:

> char *tparm(terminfo_str, p1, p2, p3, p4, p5, p6, p7, p8, p9)

The first argument must be supplied but the others need only be supplied as required. `tparm()` performs parameter substitution to a terminfo parameterized capability string. A pointer to the resultant string is then passed back to the calling routine. The following program uses *curses* to explain this:

```
#include <curses.h>
#include <term.h>

main()
{
    char *tparm();

    initscr();
    printw("Before tparm - %s\n",cursor_address);
    printw("After tparm - %s\n",tparm(cursor_address,2,15));
    refresh();
    endwin();
}
```

The idea here is to print out the capability string `cursor_address` both before and after `tparm()`. *Curses* is used because both of these strings may contain non-printable characters, and *curses* conveniently translates them into a printable form for us (see Section 3.5). If you run this program from an ansi terminal using the terminfo description discussed in Chapter 7, you should see the following on the screen:

```
Before tparm - ^[[%i%p1%d;%p2%dH
After tparm - ^[[3;16H
```

We asked `tparm()` to instantiate the `cursor_address` capability string with the parameters 2 and 15. If we had passed this string to `tputs()` it would have moved the cursor to absolute address; line 2, column 15. But notice that the resultant string passed back says line 3, column 16. This is because the capability string explicitly specifies `%i` which informs `tparm()` to add one to each parameter (Section 7.7 explains why this is so).

9.5 Cursor-addressing

Terminfo programs should place the terminal into a *cursor-addressing* mode before using capabilities which do cursor-addressing. Similarly, this mode should be turned off before exiting a terminfo program. In the previous example where we used *curses*, we didn't have to do this as the `initscr()` and `endwin()` functions did it for us. But because our `clearscreen()` function uses cursor-addressing we must explicitly set these modes if they are defined. The following example does this in `main()`:

```
#include <curses.h>
#include <term.h>

main()
{
    setupterm((char *)0, 1, (int *)0);

    if(enter_ca_mode)
        putp(enter_ca_mode);
    clearscreen();
    if(exit_ca_mode)
        putp(exit_ca_mode);
    reset_shell_mode();
}
```

9.6 Leaving terminfo

Before returning to the shell your program must restore the *tty* driver to a sane condition. This is done with `reset_shell_mode()`. This is true for shell escapes also:

```
shell_escape()
{
    reset_shell_mode();
    if(exit_ca_mode)
        putp(exit_ca_mode);
    system("/bin/sh");
```

```
    if(enter_ca_mode)
        putp(enter_ca_mode);
    reset_prog_mode();
}
```

These functions are normally used when you have modified the *tty* driver modes
within your program. For example, after calling `setupterm()` you may want to
turn echoing off with `noecho()` or turn `cbreak()` mode on. To save these
modes you call `def_prog_mode()`. Then, if you exit to the shell, you call
`rest_shell_mode()` to restore the *tty* driver to its normal working state. When
the program returns, you call `reset_prog_mode()` so that the driver is restored
to the state it was in before exiting to the shell.

9.7 Using video attributes

Two functions are provided by terminfo for managing the terminal's video
attributes:

```
vidputs(attributes, putc_function)
vidattr(attributes)
```

The `attributes` specified can be any combination of attributes defined in the
`<curses.h>` file. These functions are similar to the *curses* routines `attrset()`
and `attron()` and use the same defined constants. Attributes can be combined
in the same way using the C language OR '|' operator. The argument
`putc_function` is a pointer to a function which is used for output. This is
exactly the same as for `tputs()` and the same output routine can be used. In
much the same way as `putp()` works, `vidattr()` indirectly calls `putchar()`
with `vidputs(attributes, putchar)`. Here is a typical example using
attributes:

```
#include <curses.h>
#include <term.h>

main()
{
    setupterm((char *)0,1,(int *)0);
    vidattr(A_STANDOUT | A_UNDERLINE | A_BLINK);
    printf("Hello World\n");
    vidattr(~A_ATTRIBUTES);
    reset_shell_mode();
}
```

9.8 Functions to query the database

There are three functions which return the value of a queried description capability, and each uses a single argument which is a defined *capname* string.

tigetflag(*capname*)   This function returns 0 if the *boolean* capability is not defined for the terminal. −1 is returned if the passed capname is not a boolean capability.

tigetnum(*capname*)   This function returns −1 if the *numeric* capability is not defined for the terminal. −2 is returned if the passed capname is not a number capability.

tigetstr(*capname*)   This function returns (char *)0 if the *string* capability is not defined for the terminal. (char *)−1 is returned if the passed capname is not a string capability.

This function tests if the terminal is an 80-column screen:

```
is80columns()
{
    return(tigetnum("cols") == 80 ? TRUE : FALSE);
}
```

Don't forget to quote the string.

9.9 Termcap emulation

Terminfo also provides a set of routines which emulate the old *termcap* library, although these routines may be phased out in future releases of UNIX. They provide upward compatibility for programs that were written using the termcap library.

Although these functions are emulated by using terminfo they are fully compatible with the original termcap library. However, whereas the original library used the /etc/termcap text file, the terminfo emulation routines use compiled files in /usr/lib/terminfo. Also, the environment variable TERMINFO is used instead of TERMCAP.

The termcap emulation routines are supplied as an integral part of libcurses.a, and so no other special libraries need to be included when compiling. But if you are porting a termcap program with a makefile, you may need to software link /usr/lib/libcurses.a to /usr/lib/libtermlib.a so that the makefile does not complain that it can't find it.

The format of a termcap file is basically the same as for a terminfo description in that capabilities are described in a similar fashion. Nevertheless, there are some fundamental differences which we will discuss.

Termcap uses a different naming system for capabilities. The terminfo naming system is based on the ANSI X3.64 standard, whereas the termcap system uses a set of two-character codes. For example, the terminfo name for *cursor_address* is cup but termcap uses cm. For convenience, the Appendix cross-references the terminfo-to-termcap naming convention and describes each capability. Here is an example termcap entry for a Datamedia 1520 terminal:

```
D0|dm1520|1520|datamedia 1520:\
            :am:bs:pt:co#80:li#24:\
            :cd=^K:ce=^]:cl=^L:cm=^^%r%+ %.:\
            :ho=^Y:ku=^_:kd=^J:\
            :kl=^H:kr=^\:kh=^Y:\
            :nd=^\:up=^_:xn:ma=^\ ^_^P^YH:
```

The convention of naming a terminal is slightly different with termcap. The first name in the alias name list is always a two-character code with the first character identifying the manufacturer. The second alias is the most common name used to set in the shell environment variable TERM. The third alias is used by the UNIX command **tset**, which is found on systems that use termcap. This program is used in a similar fashion to the UNIX System V **tput** command. The last alias is a verbose description of the terminal being described. The alias line is terminated with a colon ':'; the capabilities then follow on the next line.

Similar to terminfo, termcap indents each line apart from the alias line. Also, each line of capabilities starts with a colon ':' and ends in a backslash '\', except for the last line of the description which ends with a colon. Also, capability fields described within the description are separated with a colon.

The only other major difference is the interpretation of parameterized strings and strings which use padding. Parameterized strings use a similar convention to terminfo in that the percent (%) character is treated specially. However, the % encodings are different. Table 9.1 describes the termcap % encodings.

The Datamedia 1520 needs the current line and column sent preceded by a Control-^, (that's a Control-up-hat) with the row and column offset by a blank. Note that the row and column are reversed '%r':

```
:cm=^^%r%+ %.:
```

Table 9.1

TERMCAP % ENCODED CONVERSION SPECIFICATIONS	
Sequence	*Description*
%.	Like %c in printf(3)
%+n	Like %c in printf(3) but adds the value *n* to it
%%	Outputs the % character
%>ab	Binary operation only, tests if a > b. No output is done
%r	Reverses the order of line and column
%i	Like terminfo, increments line and column position
%d	Substituted with parameter, like printf(3) %d
%2	Like printf(3) %2d for a two-digit number
%3	Like printf(3) %3d for a three-digit number
%n	Exclusive OR line and column with the octal value 0140
%B	Binary Coded Decimal (BCD) operation $(16*(value/10)) + (value\%10)$, no output
%D	Reverse coding $(value - 2 * (value\%16))$, no output (Delta Data)

Padding is specified in a string capability by placing the number of milliseconds for the delay after the equals '=' character within a definition. The delay can be either an integer value, for example '20', or an integer followed by an asterisk '*', that is, '20*'. The asterisk indicates that the padding required is proportional to the number of lines affected. Padding can be specified as a single precision real, for example — '3.5'. The following example introduces a 6-millisecond padding which is proportional to the affected line count:

```
:cm=6*^^%r%+ %.:
```

Following is an explanation of the termcap emulation routines. Where *codename* is used, it refers to a two-character termcap code which must be specified as a string:

```
tgetent(bp, name)
```
This routine looks up the termcap entry for the terminal specified in `name`. The terminfo emulation ignores `bp`, but in the original version of this routine `bp` is a pointer to an area which you must supply and which must be exactly 1024 bytes long. This area contains the entire termcap entry and must be retained

throughout the termcap program. The functions `tgetflag()`, `tgetnum()` and `tgetstr()` use an internal pointer which points to this area. If `tgetent()` finds that this area is bigger than 1024 bytes it will print a message to the screen; it will then proceed to read in the first 1024 bytes of the entry, ignoring the rest.

`char *tgetstr(codename, area)`
The string entry for the `codename` is returned. `area` is normally the area which was filled by `tgetent()`. If `area` is not a NULL pointer, then the returned string is also copied into the area pointed to by `area` and the pointer is then advanced to the first byte after the string entered. The `tputs()` function is used to output the returned string. As a side issue, the `tgetent()` emulation calls `setupterm()` and if it returns an error then `rest_shell_mode()` is called.

`tgoto(cap,column,line)`
Note that column and line are reversed — this is the only function in the library that does this. `tgoto()` works a bit like `tparm()` in that it does parameter substitution. This would normally be used for cursor-addressing. The parameters `column` and `line` are used to specify the values to be placed into the parameterized string. The string returned from `tgoto()` is also passed to `tputs()` for output.

`tgetflag(codename)`
Returns the boolean termcap entry for `"codename"`

`tgetnum(codename)`
Returns the numeric termcap entry for `"codename"`

`tputs(str, affcnt, putc)`
The termcap emulation uses the standard terminfo `tputs()` (see Section 9.4).

Here is the clear-screen program again but this time using the termcap routines.

```
#include <curses.h>
#include <term.h>


char tcapbuf[50];
main()
{
    char entry[1024];
    char *name;
    char *getenv();

    if((name = getenv("TERM")) == (char *)NULL) {
```

```
            fprintf(stderr,"TERM not set\n");
            exit(1);
    }

    if(tgetent(entry,name) == ERR) {
            fprintf(stderr,"No termcap entry found\n");
            exit(1);
    }

    clearscreen();
    exit(0);
}


clearscreen()
{
    char *p1, *p2;
    char *tgetstr();
    int my_putchar();
    int li;
    int x;

    if(p1 = tgetstr("cl",tcapbuf))
        tputs(p1,1,my_putchar);
    else if((p1 = tgetstr("ho",tcapbuf)) &&
            (p2 = tgetstr("cd",tcapbuf))) {
        tputs(p1,1,my_putchar);
        tputs(p2,1,my_putchar);
    } else if((p1 = tgetstr("cd",tcapbuf)) &&
            (p2 = tgetstr("cm",tcapbuf))) {
        tputs(tgoto(p2,0,0),1,my_putchar);
        tputs(p1,1,my_putchar);
    } else if(li = tgetnum("li")) {
        for(x = 0; x < li; x++)
            printf("\r\n");
        fflush(stdout);
    } else {
        printf("Can't do that\n");
        exit(1);
    }
}
```

```
my_putchar(c)
int c;
{
    putchar(c);
}
```

Note that for completeness this program has defined the buffer entry[1024]. However, under UNIX System V this argument is ignored by tgetent() and so it is sufficient to pass a NULL pointer.

CHAPTER 10

Curses Library

The following pages contain, in alphabetic order, a brief description of each function in the `/usr/lib/libcurses.a` library.

Many of the routines are prefixed with a special naming convention. These are usually pseudo-functions defined in `<curses.h>` and are made up from a base function:

Routines prefixed with *w* require a *window* or *pad* argument.

Routines prefixed with *p* require a *pad* argument.

Routines prefixed with *mv* imply a `move()`; these routines require *y* and *x* arguments specifying the required location to move to.

Routines prefixed with *mvw* require both a *window/pad* and *y,x* arguments. The *window* argument is supplied before the *y,x* coordinates.

In general, routines without a prefix are used specifically with *stdscr*.

The *termcap* routines `tgetent()`; `tgetflag()`; `tgetnum()`; `tgetstr()`; and `tgoto()` are emulated using the *terminfo* package. No reference to `/etc/termcap` is made.

addch()	Add a character to stdscr	addch
addstr()	Add a string to stdscr	addstr
attroff()	Turn stdscr attributes off	attron
attron()	Turn stdscr attributes on	attron
attrset()	Manipulate stdscr attributes	attron
baudrate()	Get operating speed of terminal	environ
beep()	Signal the user audibly	beep
box()	Draw a box around a window	box
can_change_color()	Test if terminal can change color	environ
cbreak()	Turn on canonical processing	cbreak
clear()	Clear stdscr to blanks	clear
clearok()	Force a clear screen	clearok
clrtobot()	Clear to bottom of screen in stdscr	clrtobot
clrtoeol()	Clear to end of line in stdscr	clrtoeol
color_content()	Obtain color content information	color_content
copywin()	Overlay/overwrite two windows	copywin
crmode()	Turn on canonical processing	cbreak
curs_set()	Modify cursor visibility	curs_set
def_prog_mode()	Default *curses* operating mode	def_prog_mode
def_shell_mode()	Default shell operating mode	def_prog_mode
del_curterm()	Deallocate space associated with TERMINAL	del_curterm
delay_output()	Cause an output delay	delay_output
delch()	Delete a character under the cursor	delch
deleteln()	Delete the current line	deleteln
delwin()	Delete a window	delwin
doupdate()	Update physical screen	doupdate
draino()	Suspend program execution	draino
echo()	Turn on input echoing	echo
echochar()	Fast character output routines for stdscr	echochar
endwin()	Exit *curses* mode	endwin
erase()	Clear stdscr to blanks	erase
erasechar()	Get *tty* driver erase character	environ
filter()	Turn on one-line video mode	filter
flash()	Signal the user visually	flash
flushinp()	Throw away pending keyboard input	flushinp
flushok()	Flush the standard output descriptor	flushok
garbagedlines()	Throw away lines in a window	garbagedlines
getbegyx()	Query window position	getyx
getch()	Read a character into stdscr	getch
getmaxyx()	Query window position	getyx
getstr()	Read string into stdscr	getstr
getsyx()	Get the current screen coordinates	getsyx
getyx()	Get current cursor position	getyx
halfdelay()	Keyboard input timeout	halfdelay

`has_colors()`	Test if terminal supports color ....environ	
`has_ic()`	Test terminal insert/delete char capability...............environ	
`has_il()`	Test terminal insert/delete char capability...............environ	
`idlok()`	Enable/disable insert/delete-line capability ....idlok	
`inch()`	Get character under the cursor in stdscr ....inch	
`init_color()`	Change the definition of a color................................init_color	
`init_pair()`	Change the definition of a color-pair.......................init_pair	
`initscr()`	*Curses* initialization and start up routine................initscr	
`insch()`	Insert a character into stdscr....................................insch	
`insertln()`	Insert line above the current one in stdscr................insertln	
`intrflush()`	Flush keyboard input queue on interrupt.................intrflush	
`isendwin()`	Test if endwin() has been called...............................environ	
`keyname()`	Return string containing key name..........................environ	
`keypad()`	Enable/Disable the terminal's function key pad........keypad	
`killchar()`	Get *tty* driver kill character....................................environ	
`leaveok()`	Leave cursor at the current location after a change....leaveok	
`longname()`	Get long name of terminal ....environ	
`meta()`	Turn on/off 8-bit input processing ....meta	
`move()`	Change the current Y,X coordinates of stdscr ....move	
`mvaddch()`	Move then add a character to stdscr..........................addch	
`mvaddstr()`	Add a string to window ....addstr	
`mvcur()`	Low-level cursor-addressing.....................................mvcur	
`mvgetch()`	Move then read character into stdscr........................getch	
`mvgetstr()`	Move then read string into stdscr.............................getstr	
`mvinch()`	Move then get character under cursor in stdscr..........inch	
`mvinsch()`	Move then insert a character into stdscr ....insch	
`mvprintw()`	Move then print formatted output to stdscr..............printw	
`mvscanw()`	Move then read formatted string into stdscr ....scanw	
`mvwaddch()`	Move then add a character to window ....addch	
`mvwaddstr()`	Move then add a string to window...........................addstr	
`mvwgetch()`	Move then read character into window ....getch	
`mvwgetstr()`	Move then read string into window...........................getstr	
`mvwin()`	Move a window to a new location ....mvwin	
`mvwinch()`	Move then get character under cursor in window.......inch	
`mvwinsch()`	Move then insert a character into window ....insch	
`mvwprintw()`	Move then print formatted string to a window..........printw	
`mvwscanw()`	Move then read formatted string into window ....scanw	
`napms()`	Put process to sleep for milliseconds........................napms	
`newpad()`	Create a new pad ....newpad	
`newterm()`	Alternative *curses* initialization function..................newterm	
`newwin()`	Create a new window...newwin	
`nl()`	Turn on new-line mode..nl	
`nocbreak()`	Turn off canonical processing ....cbreak	
`nocrmode()`	Turn off canonical processing ....cbreak	

nodelay()	Toggle on/off input delay	nodelay
noecho()	Turn off input echoing	echo
nonl()	Turn off new-line mode	nl
noraw()	Turn off raw mode	raw
notimeout()	Toggle internal input timer	notimeout
overlay()	Overlay window non-destructively	overlay
overwrite()	Overlay window destructively	overwrite
pair_content()	Obtain color-pair content information	pair_content
pechochar()	Fast character output routine	echochar
pnoutrefresh()	Update (refresh) a pad	prefresh
prefresh()	Update (refresh) a pad on the screen	prefresh
printw()	Print formatted output to stdscr	printw
putp()	Low-level output routine	tputs
raw()	Turn on raw mode	raw
refresh()	Update the terminal screen	refresh
reset_prog_mode()	Reset *curses* mode	reset_prog_mode
reset_shell_mode()	Reset shell mode	reset_prog_mode
resetty()	Restore terminal driver modes	savetty
restartterm()	Re-initialize *curses* environment	restartterm
ripoffline()	Reduce the size of the screen by one line	ripoffline
savetty()	Save terminal driver modes	savetty
scanw()	Read formatted string from stdscr	scanw
scr_dump()	Save *curses* virtual screen	scr_dump
scr_init()	Initialize after restoring virtual screen	scr_dump
scr_restore()	Restore *curses* virtual screen	scr_dump
scroll()	Scroll window up a line	scroll
scrollok()	Toggle window scrolling	scrollok
set_curterm()	Set the current terminfo environment	set_curterm
set_term()	Alternative *curses* initialization function	newterm
setscrreg()	Preset scrolling region for stdscr	setscrreg
setsyx()	Set current screen coordinates	getsyx
setupterm()	Low-level terminfo initialization	setupterm
slk_clear()	Clear soft label	slk_clear
slk_init()	Initialize soft labels	slk_clear
slk_label()	Get contents of label	slk_clear
slk_noutrefresh()	Update without refresh, a soft label	slk_clear
slk_refresh()	Refresh labels	slk_clear
slk_restore()	Restore soft label	slk_clear
slk_set()	Set up soft label	slk_clear
slk_touch()	Touch all soft labels	slk_clear
standend()	Disable standout mode on stdscr	standout
standout()	Enable standout mode on stdscr	standout
start_color()	Initialize and setup *curses* for color mode	start_color
subpad()	Create a subpad	subwin

`subwin()`	Create a sub-window	subwin
`tgetent()`	Low-level termcap initialization	tgetent
`tgetflag()`	Low-level termcap query.......................................	tgetent
`tgetnum()`	Low-level termcap query.......................................	tgetent
`tgetstr()`	Low-level termcap query.......................................	tgetent
`tgoto()`	Low-level termcap cursor-addressing........................	tgoto
`tigetflag()`	Low-level terminfo query	tigetflag
`tigetnum()`	Low-level terminfo query	tigetflag
`tigetstr()`	Low-level terminfo query	tigetflag
`touchline()`	Update the whole line	touchline
`touchoverlap()`	Update portions of overlapping windows	touchoverlap
`touchwin()`	Update the whole window	touchwin
`tparm()`	Low-level terminfo parameter substitution	tparm
`tputs()`	Low-level terminfo/termcap output routine..............	tputs
`traceoff()`	Turn off debugging trace output	traceon
`traceon()`	Turn on debugging trace output	traceon
`typeahead()`	Check for input typeahead	typeahead
`unctrl()`	Get string representation of character	unctrl
`ungetch()`	Push character back onto *curses* input queue............	ungetch
`vidattr()`	Low-level terminfo video attribute manipulation	vidputs
`vidputs()`	Low-level terminfo video attribute manipulation	vidputs
`waddch()`	Add character to window	addch
`waddstr()`	Add string to window...	addstr
`wattroff()`	Turn window attributes off	attron
`wattron()`	Turn window attributes on	attron
`wattrset()`	Manipulate window attributes................................	attron
`wclear()`	Clear window to blanks	clear
`wclrtobot()`	Clear to bottom of the window...............................	clrtobot
`wclrtoeol()`	Clear to end of line in window	clrtoeol
`wdelch()`	Delete character under cursor in window	delch
`wdeleteln()`	Delete current line in window	deleteln
`wechochar()`	Fast character output routine for windows	echochar
`werase()`	Clear window to blanks	erase
`wgetch()`	Read character into window...................................	getch
`wgetstr()`	Read string into window.......................................	getstr
`winch()`	Get character under cursor in window	inch
`winsch()`	Insert character into window	insch
`winsertln()`	Insert line above current one in window...................	insertln
`wmove()`	Change current y,x coordinates in window...............	move
`wnoutrefresh()`	Update *curses* virtual screen...................................	wnoutrefresh
`wprintw()`	Print formatted output into window........................	printw
`wrefresh()`	Update the terminal screen....................................	refresh
`wscanw()`	Read formatted string into window	scanw
`wsetscrreg()`	Preset scrolling region for window	setscrreg

NAME

addch, waddch — Add a character to a window.

SYNOPSIS

```
#include <curses.h>

int addch(ch)
chtype ch;

int waddch(win, ch)
WINDOW *win;
chtype ch;

int mvaddch(y, x, ch)
int y;
int x;
chtype ch;

int mvwaddch(win, y, x, ch)
WINDOW *win;
int y;
int x;
chtype ch;
```

DESCRIPTION

waddch() adds the character ch to the specified window win at the current y,x coordinates. If attributes are currently set, or attributes are OR'ed into ch, the character is added to the window with the specified attributes.

Except for the following characters, the character ch is added to the window and the current x coordinate is advanced by 1.

new-line (\n)   If new-line mapping is on, the current line will be cleared to the end, and the current y,x coordinates will be set to the beginning of the next line. If new-line mapping is off, the coordinates are set to the same x coordinate, the y coordinate is set to the following line.

return (\r)   Sets the current x coordinate to the beginning of the current line, emulating a carriage return without line feed.

tab (\t)   A tab is expanded into spaces in the normal tabstop positions of every eight characters.

[addch]

backspace (\b)   If the current x coordinate is greater than 0,
                            the backspace character decrements the current
                            x coordinate by 1.

non-printable   If ch is any other non-printable character, it
                            will be replaced with a printable version (as
                            processed by the function unctrl()) preceded
                            by the character '^'.

If required, video attributes can be combined by ORing the required
attributes into the character to be added (see attron()).

RETURNS
waddch() returns ERR if adding the character would scroll the screen
illegally. Otherwise, OK is returned.

NOTE
Functions addch(), mvaddch() and mvwaddch() are pseudo-
functions defined in <curses.h>. addch() and mvaddch() are
specifically set up for use with stdscr.

SEE ALSO
unctrl(), nl(), attron()

[addch]

NAME
        addstr, waddstr — Add a string to a window.

SYNOPSIS
        #include <curses.h>

        int addstr(str)
        char *str;

        int waddstr(win, str)
        WINDOW *win;
        char *str;

        int mvaddstr(y, x, str)
        int y;
        int x;
        char *str;

        int mvwaddstr(win, y, x, str)
        WINDOW *win;
        int y;
        int x;
        char *str;

DESCRIPTION
        waddstr() adds a string pointed to by str to the specified window
        win at the current y,x coordinates. str must be a NULL-terminated
        string. waddstr() recursively calls waddch() on the window, until a
        terminating NULL character is reached.

RETURNS
        waddstr() returns ERR if adding a character to the window would
        scroll the screen illegally. In this case, it will put on as much as it can.
        OK is returned if no errors are encountered.

NOTE
        functions addstr(), mvaddstr() and mvwaddstr() are pseudo-
        functions defined in <curses.h>. Also addstr() and mvaddstr()
        are specifically set up for use with stdscr.

SEE ALSO
        waddch()

                                                            [addstr]

NAME

attron, attroff, attrset — Manipulate window attributes.

SYNOPSIS

```
#include <curses.h>

int attron(attrs)
chtype attrs;

int wattron(win, attrs)
WINDOW *win;
chtype attrs;

int attroff(attrs)
chtype attrs;

int wattroff(win,attrs)
WINDOW *win;
chtype attrs;

int attrset(attrs)
chtype attrs;

int wattrset(win,attrs)
WINDOW *win;
chtype attrs;
```

DESCRIPTION

These routines manipulate the current attributes of the named window win. Attributes (attrs) may be any combination of the A_ or ACS_ constants defined in the header file <curses.h>. Constants may be OR'ed together using the C logical OR '|' operator to turn on (wattron) or off (wattroff) the attributes desired. The function wattrset() sets the current attributes of the window win to attrs, whereas the functions wattron() and wattroff() turn on and off attributes respectively without affecting any other current attribute settings. Note that the statement wattrset(win,0) turns off all attributes.

The current attributes of a window are applied to all characters written into a window either directly or indirectly with waddch(). Attributes remain the property of each individual character written, and move with the character during scrolling, and so on. Wherever possible the package will apply these attributes when requested to do so; however, if the terminal is not capable of rendering the character in such a way then the request is ignored.

RETURNS

The package assumes that the attributes requested are supported by the terminal in use. Therefore all these functions return OK regardless.

NOTE

The functions `attron()`, `attroff()` and `attrset()` are pseudo-functions set up for use with `stdscr`.

These functions were introduced with the release of System V.

SEE ALSO

`standout()`, `standend()`

[attron]

NAME

beep — Signal the user.

SYNOPSIS

```
void beep()
```

DESCRIPTION

This routine signals the user at the terminal by sounding an audible alarm. If this is not possible the package will try to make the terminal screen flash. If neither is possible nothing will happen. Almost all terminals are able to sound a bell, usually by sending the sequence 0x07 (Control-G) to the terminal, but not all terminals can make the screen flash.

RETURNS

Void — No return value.

SEE ALSO

```
flash()
```

NAME

box — Draw a box around a window.

SYNOPSIS

```
#include <curses.h>

void box(win, vert, hor)
WINDOW *win;
chtype vert;
chtype hor;
```

DESCRIPTION

This function draws a box around the window pointed to by `win`, using the character `vert` to draw the vertical sides of the box, and `hor` to draw the horizontal sides.

If either of `vert` or `hor` are 0, then `box()` uses the default characters '|' for vertical, and '-' for horizontal respectively.

If the window is not allowed to scroll and the window encompasses the lower right-hand corner of the terminal screen, the lower right-hand corner is left blank to avoid scrolling the terminal.

RETURNS

Void — No return value.

NOTE

System V.3 versions of *curses* use the line drawing glyphs of the Alternate Character Set as default characters to draw the box.

CAVEAT

The window is touched with `touchwin()`, which effectively makes *curses* think the whole window has been updated.

NAME

cbreak, nocbreak, crmode, nocrmode — Turn on or off canonical input processing.

SYNOPSIS

```
#include <curses.h>

void cbreak()

void nocbreak()

crmode()

nocrmode()
```

DESCRIPTION

The functions `cbreak()` and `nocbreak()` turn off and on canonical (erase and kill) input processing respectively. These functions perform low-level I/O control setting of the terminal driver.

In *cbreak*-mode, characters typed at the keyboard are made available to the *curses* routines as soon as they are entered without being processed or buffered by the terminal driver. However, unlike *raw*-mode, the Interrupt and Quit keys, and the following control codes, continue to be processed by the driver:

^S   Stops the screen output; this has the same effect as the keyboard Scroll-Lock.

^Q   Starts the screen output; this has the inverse effect of ^S.

The function `nocbreak()` turns canonical processing back on. This is the default mode set when *curses* is started with `initscr()`.

`crmode()` and `nocrmode()`, now unsupported *curses* features, have been replaced with `cbreak()` and `nocbreak()` respectively.

RETURNS

Void — No return value.

NOTE

Pre-System V versions of *curses* and current Berkeley Distributions implemented `crmode()` and `nocrmode()` as pseudo-functions defined in `<curses.h>`

SEE ALSO

raw(), noraw(), halfdelay()

[cbreak]

NAME

clear, wclear — Clear a window to blanks.

SYNOPSIS

```
#include <curses.h>

int clear()

int wclear(win)
WINDOW *win;
```

DESCRIPTION

wclear() resets the entire window pointed to by win to blanks. It does this by calling the function werase() to erase the contents then sets the current y,x coordinates of the window to 0,0.

   If win is a full window the size of the terminal screen, then wclear() will set the WINDOW variable win->clear to TRUE. This has the effect of sending a clear-screen sequence to the terminal on the next call to wrefresh() on that window.

RETURNS

wclear() returns OK regardless.

NOTE

The function clear() is a pseudo-function set up for use with stdscr.

SEE ALSO

erase()

NAME

clearok — Force a clear screen before a refresh.

SYNOPSIS

```
#include <curses.h>

void clearok(win, boolf)
WINDOW *win;
bool boolf;
```

DESCRIPTION

clearok() sets the clear flag (win->_clear) for the window pointed
to by win. If boolf is TRUE, this will force a clear-screen sequence to
be sent to the terminal screen before completely redrawing it again on
the next call to wrefresh() on that window, or stop it from doing so if
boolf is FALSE.

   clearok() works only on windows that are the size of the terminal
screen and does not alter the contents of the window. If win is
curscr, the next call to wrefresh() will send a clear-screen sequence
to the terminal screen, even if the window passed to wrefresh() is not
the size of a screen.

RETURNS

Void — No return value.

NOTE

Some implementations of *curses* define clearok() as a pseudo-
function in <curses.h>.

[clearok]

NAME

clrtobot, wclrtobot — Clear to the bottom of the window.

SYNOPSIS

#include <curses.h>

int clrtobot()

int wclrtobot(win)
WINDOW *win;

DESCRIPTION

The window pointed to by win is wiped clear and blanked from the current y,x coordinates to the bottom inclusive. wclrtobot() does not force a clear-screen sequence to be sent to the terminal screen on the next call to wrefresh().

RETURNS

System V.3 returns OK regardless. System V.2 has no return value.

NOTE

The function clrtobot() is a pseudo-function set up for use with stdscr and is defined in the <curses.h> file.

[clrtobot]

NAME

clrtoeol, wclrtoeol — Clear to the end of line.

SYNOPSIS

```
#include <curses.h>

int clrtoeol()

int wclrtoeol(win)
WINDOW *win;
```

DESCRIPTION

wclrtoeol() clears the current line on the window pointed to by win to blanks from the current y,x coordinates to the end of the line inclusive.

RETURNS

System V.3 returns OK regardless. System V.2 has no return value.

NOTE

The function clrtoeol() is a pseudo-function set up for use with stdscr and is defined in the <curses.h> file.

[clrtoeol]

NAME

color_content — Obtain color content information.

SYNOPSIS

```
#include <curses.h>

int color_content(color, red, green, blue)
int color;
short *red;
short *green;
short *blue;
```

DESCRIPTION

This routine obtains the current color-content information of a given color.

The routine uses four arguments: the `color` number, which must be a value between 0 (zero) and COLORS −1, and the addresses of three short integers for storing the obtained information of the color components `red`, `green` and `blue`. The function stores the current values at these addresses passed. The values range from 0 (no color component) to 1000 (the maximum color component).

The global variable COLORS defined in `<curses.h>` is initialized by the function `start_color()`.

RETURNS

`color_content()` returns ERR if the color is out of range or does not exist, or if the terminal cannot redefine color definitions. Otherwise, OK is returned.

NOTE

This function was introduced with the release of System V.3.2.

SEE ALSO

start_color(), init_pair(), init_color(), pair_content(), environ()

NAME

copywin — Overlay/overwrite a part of a window on top of another.

SYNOPSIS

```
#include <curses.h>

int copywin(Srcwin, Dstwin, minRowSrc,
    minColSrc, minRowDst, minColDst,
    maxRowDst, maxColDst, overlay)
WINDOW *Srcwin;
WINDOW *Dstwin;
int minRowSrc;
int minColSrc;
int minRowDst;
int minColDst;
int maxRowDst;
int maxColDst;
int overlay;
```

DESCRIPTION

This routine is similar to the functions overlay() and overwrite(). However, copywin() allows you to specify what portion of the source window is to be copied, and also what portion of the destination window will be affected. Also, unlike overlay() and overwrite() neither of the windows have to overlap for the copy to take place.

Srcwin specifies the source window to copy from, and Dstwin specifies the destination window that will be affected.

The argument overlay specifies the effect of the copy. If this argument is TRUE, then the copy is done non-destructively. That is, blanks on the source window leave the contents of the space on the destination window untouched. If overlay is FALSE then blanks on the source window will become blanks on the destination window.

The arguments minRowSrc,minColSrc specify the upper left-hand corner of the rectangular portion of the source window to be copied.

Arguments minRowDst,minColDst and maxRowDst,maxColDst specify the rectangular portion of the destination window which will be affected. Arguments minRowDst,minColDst specify the upper left-hand corner of the copy area, and maxRowDst,maxColDst specify the bottom right-hand corner of the copy area.

RETURNS

copywin() returns ERR if an attempt is made to copy to the virtual screen curscr, or if an attempt to copy over the edge of the destination window is made. OK is returned otherwise.

[copywin]

NOTE

This routine was introduced with the release of System V.3.

SEE ALSO

overlay(), overwrite()

[copywin]

NAME

curs_set — Modify the cursor visibility.

SYNOPSIS

```
int curs_set(visibility)
int visibility;
```

DESCRIPTION

This function changes the style of the cursor. The cursor can be made to be invisible, normal, or highly visible by setting `visibility` to `0,1` or `2` respectively. If the requested visibility is not possible, then *curses* will try to use normal visibility.

RETURNS

`curs_set` returns the current cursor visibility value.

NOTE

This function was introduced with the release of System V.3.

NAME

>   def_prog_mode, def_shell_mode — Save current terminal modes.

SYNOPSIS

>   `void def_prog_mode()`
>
>   `void def_shell_mode()`

DESCRIPTION

>   These routines provide a mechanism for saving the current terminal driver line discipline modes in an internal `termio(7)` structure for later use by the functions `reset_prog_mode()` and `reset_shell_mode()`.
>
>   The function `def_prog_mode()` saves the current *in-curses* state, while the function `def_shell_mode()` saves the current *out-of-curses* state. Note that this is done automatically by `initscr()` and `setupterm()`.

RETURNS

>   Void — No return value.

NOTE

>   These functions were introduced with the release of System V.

SEE ALSO

>   `reset_prog_mode()`,   `reset_shell_mode()`,   `savetty()`, `resetty()`, `initscr()`, `setupterm()`
>
>   `termio(7)` in the UNIX System V Programmer's Reference Manual.

[def_prog_mode]

NAME

del_curterm — Deallocate space associated with TERMINAL.

SYNOPSIS

```
#include <term.h>

int del_curterm(oldterminal)
TERMINAL *oldterminal;
```

DESCRIPTION

This low-level terminfo routine relinquishes the storage associated with
the `TERMINAL` structure `oldterminal` and makes it available for
further use. The space was presumably allocated by `setupterm()`.

Be aware that if `oldterminal` is a pointer to the controlling
`TERMINAL` structure, then references to this pointer may be to
unassigned memory locations.

RETURNS

This function returns `ERR` if `oldterminal` is a NULL pointer, or else
`OK` is returned.

NOTE

This function was introduced with the release of System V.3.

SEE ALSO

`setupterm()`, `set_curterm()`

[del_curterm]

NAME

delay_output — Cause an output delay.

SYNOPSIS

```
int delay_output(ms)
int ms;
```

DESCRIPTION

This function causes a delay specified in milliseconds (ms) in the output but does not necessarily suspend the processor. For applications requiring execution suspension with a time resolution of 1/10th of a second or less, this function should not be used.

delay_output() causes a pause in the displayed output, but because padding characters may be sent to the terminal, it is not recommended that the pause period be more than 1/2 of a second, especially at high baud rates.

RETURNS

delay_output() returns ERR if the current baud rate of the terminal is less than or equal to zero. Otherwise OK is returned.

NOTE

On some systems this function has no effect.

This function was introduced with the release of System V.

SEE ALSO

napms(), draino()

CAVEAT

Transmitting pad characters loads the system and slows many terminals down. Also, due to possible system delays, the actual pause time may be prolonged even further.

[delay_output]

NAME
delch, wdelch — Delete a character under the cursor.

SYNOPSIS
```
#include <curses.h>

int delch()

int wdelch(win)
WINDOW *win;

int mvdelch(y, x)
int y;
int x;

int mvwdelch(win, y, x)
WINDOW *win;
int y;
int x;
```

DESCRIPTION
wdelch() deletes the character under the cursor at the current y,x coordinates on the window pointed to by win. Each character after it on the current line is shifted left, and the last character becomes blank. The cursor position remains unchanged.

RETURNS
wdelch() returns OK regardless.

NOTE
The functions delch(), mvdelch() and mvwdelch() are pseudo-functions defined in <curses.h>. Also delch() and mvdelch() are specifically set up for use with stdscr.

[delch]

NAME

   deleteln, wdeleteln — Delete the current line.

SYNOPSIS

   #include <curses.h>

   void deleteln()

   void wdeleteln(win)
   WINDOW *win;

DESCRIPTION

   wdeleteln() deletes the current line in the window pointed to by win.
   Each line below the current line in win is shifted up a line, and the last
   line is cleared. The current y,x coordinates are unchanged.

RETURNS

   Void — No return value.

NOTE

   The function deleteln() is a pseudo-function set up for use with
   stdscr and is defined in the <curses.h> file.

[deleteln]

NAME

        delwin — Delete a window.

SYNOPSIS

        `#include <curses.h>`

        `void delwin(win)`
        `WINDOW *win;`

DESCRIPTION

        This routine entirely deletes the named window or pad `win`, and frees up all memory associated with it.

        Once a window has been deleted it will not be possible to reference any sub-windows that were associated with it; therefore sub-windows should be deleted first before calling `delwin()` on the main window.

RETURNS

        Void — No return value.

NAME
doupdate — Update physical terminal screen.

SYNOPSIS
```
int doupdate()
```

DESCRIPTION
This routine compares the virtual screen (curscr) to the physical screen. It updates the parts of the physical screen that have changed since last being updated.

The function wrefresh() does this automatically after calling wnoutrefresh(win), which copies the contents of the named window into the curscr virtual screen first.

If many windows are to be updated at the same time it is more efficient to call wnoutrefresh() on each window and then make a single call to doupdate(). This method is not only more efficient than individual calls to wrefresh(), but also has a more pleasing effect, since only a single burst of output is made rather than individual bursts of output per window.

RETURNS
doupdate() returns the number of characters transmitted to the physical terminal screen.

NOTE
This function was introduced with the release of System V.

SEE ALSO
wnoutrefresh(), pnoutrefresh(), wrefresh(), prefresh()

NAME

> draino — Suspend program execution.

SYNOPSIS

```
int draino(ms)
int ms;
```

DESCRIPTION

> This routine inserts a delay into program execution and suspends the program until the amount of time specified in `ms` (milliseconds) has elapsed. `draino()` provides a higher-resolution delay time than that of the standard `sleep(3)` library call, which has a minimum sleep resolution time of 1 second.

RETURNS

> `draino()` returns `ERR` if the function is not supported. Otherwise `OK` is returned.

NOTE

> This function was introduced with the release of System V, but since not all systems provide kernel support for this function, it may not work on all implementations.

SEE ALSO

> `delay_output()`, `napms()`
>
> `sleep(3)` in the UNIX System V Programmer's Reference Manual

NAME

echo, noecho — Turn on and off echoing of input characters.

SYNOPSIS

```
#include <curses.h>

void echo()

void noecho()
```

DESCRIPTION

echo() and noecho() set the terminal driver duplex mode. If *curses* is in *echo*-mode (default), the driver is set into **full-duplex** mode. Characters are echoed back to the terminal screen as they are received.

In *noecho*-mode, the driver is set into **half-duplex** mode. Characters, although received from the terminal, are not echoed back to it and so are not displayed.

RETURNS

Void — No return value.

NOTE

Pre-System V and BSD versions of *curses* implement these routines as pseudo-functions defined in `<curses.h>`

[echo]

NAME

echochar, wechochar, pechochar — Fast character output routines.

SYNOPSIS

```
#include <curses.h>

int echochar(ch)
chtype ch;

int wechochar(win, ch)
WINDOW *win;
chtype ch;

int pechochar(pad, ch)
WINDOW *pad;
chtype ch;
```

DESCRIPTION

These routines provide a method by which a non-control character can be echoed to a window or pad. They will accept control characters, but when they are used with non-control characters (for which they have been specifically designed), they by-pass much of the internal *curses* overhead and provide a considerable performance gain over their equivalent routines.

Functionally, `echochar()` is equivalent to a call to `addch()` followed by a call to `refresh()`. This function is a pseudo-function defined in the `<curses.h>` file, and has been specifically set up for use with `stdscr`. The function `wechochar()`, however, is provided for use with another window of choice specified by the argument `win`, and is equivalent to a call to `waddch()` followed by a call to `wrefresh()`. Similarly, the function `pechochar()` is equivalent to a call to `waddch()` followed by a call to `prefresh()`, and is provided for use with pads.

The character `ch` is of type `chtype` and is added to the window at the current y,x coordinates. If attributes are currently set on the working window, or attributes are OR'ed into `ch`, the character is then added with the specified attributes.

RETURNS

These functions return the total number of characters that were actually required to add the specified character to the window. Control characters may require more than one character output (see `unctrl()`). ERR is returned if it is not possible to add the character to

[echochar]

the window, or if adding the character would make the screen scroll illegally.

NOTE

When using these functions it is not necessary to call `wrefresh()` on the updated window, as this is done internally.

These functions were introduced with the release of System V.3.

SEE ALSO

unctrl(), addch()

[echochar]

NAME
endwin — Exit *curses* mode.

SYNOPSIS
```
void endwin()
```

DESCRIPTION
This routine is called before exiting or escaping from a *curses* program. endwin() attempts to restore terminal modes from an *in-curses* mode to an *out-of-curses* (*sane*) mode. It then moves the cursor to the lower left-hand corner of the terminal screen and renders the terminal into its proper non-visual mode.

If the in-*curses* mode is to be resumed — for example, after a temporary escape, the wrefresh() or doupdate() functions may be called to restore the terminal and program into an in-*curses* mode.

RETURNS
Void — No return value.

SEE ALSO
```
reset_shell_mode()
```

NAME

environ — *Curses* environment query functions.

SYNOPSIS

```
char erasechar()

char killchar()

char *longname()

int has_ic()

int has_il()

int has_colors()

int can_change_color()

int baudrate()

int isendwin()

char *keyname(key)
int key;
```

DESCRIPTION

These functions provide a platform by which the programmer can query the *curses* environment.

erasechar()	The current *tty* driver *erase* character is returned.
killchar()	The current *tty* driver *line-kill* character is returned.
longname()	Returns a pointer to a static area ttytype containing a long description of the current terminal name. The static area is overwritten by each call to newterm() or setupterm(), but it is not restored by set_term(). Therefore the contents of this static area should be saved locally between calls to newterm() or setupterm(). The static area is restricted to

[environ]

128 characters and is set up by either
`newterm()`, `setupterm()` or `initscr()`.

`has_ic()` This routine returns TRUE if the current terminal has insert/delete character capabilities (defined in the terminal's terminfo entry). Otherwise ERR is returned.

`has_il()` This routine returns TRUE if the current terminal has insert/delete line capabilities or if it can emulate them using scrolling regions. Otherwise ERR is returned. This can be used to see if it is worth using `scrollok()` to turn on physical scrolling.

`has_colors()` Returns TRUE if the current terminal supports and can manipulate colors. Otherwise ERR is returned.

`can_change_color()` Returns TRUE if the current terminal supports colors and it is possible to change their definition. Otherwise ERR is returned.

`baudrate()` This routine returns the current terminal's baud rate setting. For example, 9600 is returned if the terminal's current baud rate is set to 9600 baud.

`isendwin()` Returns TRUE if the function `endwin()` has been called.

`keyname(key)` Returns a pointer to a character string containing a symbolic name corresponding to that specified in the argument key. key may be any key returned from `wgetch()`.

The pointer returned from `keyname()` may point to a static area. If subsequent calls to `keyname()` are required, the contents of the pointer should be saved before calling `keyname()` again.

NOTE

The routines `has_ic()` and `has_il()` were introduced with the release of System V.2.

The routines `isendwin()` and `keyname()` were introduced with the release of System V.3.

[environ]

The routines `has_colors()` and `can_change_color()` were introduced with the release of System V.3.2.

The routines `erasechar()` and `killchar()` do not exist on some versions of UNIX System III.

Pre-System V and Berkeley versions of *curses* use different semantics for the function `longname()`:

```
longname(termbuf, name)
char *termbuf;
char *name;
```

The character pointer `termbuf` points to an area containing the *termcap* description of the current terminal. The area was presumably filled by the *termcap* routine `tgetent()`. The character pointer `name` is filled in with the (long) full name of the terminal described by the termcap entry; the area it points to is assumed to be big enough to hold the data. On these systems the current terminal name is also stored in a global variable `ttytype` which is defined in `<curses.h>`, and this function has no significant return value.

The function `baudrate()` also exists on late Berkeley versions of *curses*; however, its return value is a system-dependent constant defined in the include file `<sys/tty.h>` which is automatically included in `<curses.h>`.

SEE ALSO
`set_term()`, `newterm()`, `initscr()`, `scrollok()`, `tgetent()`, `endwin()`

NAME

erase, werase — Clear window to blanks.

SYNOPSIS

```
#include <curses.h>

void erase()

void werase(win)
WINDOW *win;
```

DESCRIPTION

werase() resets the entire window pointed to by win to blanks, without setting the clear flag. This function is analogous to wclear(), except that it does not cause a clear-screen sequence when wrefresh() is next called.

RETURNS

Void — No return value.

NOTE

The function erase() is a pseudo-function set up for use with stdscr and is defined in the <curses.h> file.

SEE ALSO

clear()

NAME
>   filter — Turn on one-line video mode.

SYNOPSIS
>   void filter()

DESCRIPTION
>   This routine must be called before initscr() or newterm(),
>   otherwise the internal data structures may be set up incorrectly. It is
>   used for *curses* programs that are filters. Its purpose is to arrange
>   *curses* to think that there is a 1-line screen and so does not use any
>   terminal capabilities that assume the current cursor line position.
>   Consequently the screen is not cleared on initialization.

RETURNS
>   Void — No return value.

NOTE
>   Certain terminals will make initscr() and newterm() fail if
>   filter() is not called first.
>
>   This function was introduced with the release of System V.3.

SEE ALSO
>   initscr(), newterm()

NAME

flash — Signal the user visually.

SYNOPSIS

```
void flash()
```

DESCRIPTION

This routine signals the user at the terminal by making the terminal screen flash. If this is not possible the package will try to make the terminal sound an audible alarm. If neither is possible nothing will happen. Almost all terminals are able to sound a bell, usually by sending the sequence 0x07 (Control-G) to the terminal, but not all terminals can make the screen flash.

RETURNS

Void — No return value.

SEE ALSO

```
beep()
```

NAME

flushinp — Throw away any pending keyboard input.

SYNOPSIS

```
void flushinp()
```

DESCRIPTION

This function instructs *curses* to throw away and ignore any pending keyboard input (typeahead) that has not yet been read by the program. Before returning, flushinp() calls doupdate() so that *curses* can catch up with any input that may have come from the keyboard during its execution.

RETURNS

Void — No return value.

SEE ALSO

doupdate()

[flushinp]

NAME

flushok — Flush the standard output descriptor.

SYNOPSIS

```
#include <curses.h>

flushok(win, boolf)
WINDOW *win;
int boolf;
```

DESCRIPTION

This pseudo-function was dropped from the *curses* package with the release of System V, but it still exists in Berkeley Distributions and is defined in `<curses.h>`.

Its purpose is to perform an `fflush()` on the `stdout` channel. If `boolf` is `TRUE` then `wrefresh()` will perform the flush (default) when next called.

NAME

    garbagedlines — Throw-away lines in a window.

SYNOPSIS

```
#include <curses.h>

void garbagedlines(win, begy, numlines)
WINDOW *win;
int begy;
int numlines;
```

DESCRIPTION

    This routine indicates to *curses* that the number of lines `numlines` starting at and inclusive of `begy` are to be discarded and replaced before adding any more data into them. It is normally used for programs such as editors which require a command to redraw a single line if it becomes garbaged in some way (perhaps by line interference in which case redrawing the entire screen would be subject to even more noise).

RETURNS

    Void — No return value.

NOTE

    This routine was introduced with the release of System V.3.

[garbagedlines]

NAME

getch, wgetch — Read a character from the terminal.

SYNOPSIS

```
#include <curses.h>

int getch()

int wgetch(win)
WINDOW *win;

mvgetch(y, x)
int y;
int x;

mvwgetch(win, y, x)
WINDOW *win;
int y;
int x;
```

DESCRIPTION

The function wgetch() reads in a character from the terminal associated with the window win. Normally the program will hang until a character has been entered if in cbreak() mode, or after the first new-line if in nocbreak() mode. However, on System V.3 it is possible to set a timeout (see halfdelay()) to cause wgetch() to return after a specified timeout period.

Unless echo has been turned off with noecho(), the character returned will also be echoed into the designated window win.

RETURNS

It is important to test wgetch's return value as an int and not a char, because it can return meta characters. If keypad(win,TRUE) has been called on the window and a function key is typed, wgetch() will return a token value representing the function key typed, rather than the sequence of raw characters the function key would normally output; this value may be greater than 256.

On System V.3, if the keyboard sends a character that could be the beginning of a function key sequence (such as the escape character) then wgetch() will set a timer. If the remainder of the sequence is not received within this designated time, the character will be returned, otherwise the token value representing the function key (defined in <curses.h> beginning with KEY_) will be returned. On some

[getch]

terminals this may cause a delay (if the user presses the escape key) before control is returned to the program, but it is possible to turn this timer off (see `notimeout()`).

If `nodelay(win,TRUE)` has been called on the window and no input is waiting, the value `ERR` is returned, or else the value of the character, meta character or function key token is returned.

NOTE

functions `getch()`, `mvgetch()` and `mvwgetch()` are pseudo-functions defined in `<curses.h>`. `getch()` and `mvgetch()` are specifically set up for use with `stdscr`.

SEE ALSO

`cbreak()`, `nocbreak()`, `keypad()`, `notimeout()`, `nodelay()`, `echo()`, `meta()`, `noecho()`

`tty(7)` in the UNIX System V Programmer's Reference Manual

CAVEAT

Do not use both `nocbreak()` and `echo()` at the same time when using `wgetch()`. Depending on the state of the terminal driver (see `tty(7)`), the program may produce undesirable results when a character is typed at the keyboard.

[getch]

NAME

getstr, wgetstr — Read a string into a window.

SYNOPSIS

```
#include <curses.h>

int getstr(str)
char *str;

int wgetstr(win, str)
WINDOW *win;
char *str;

int mvgetstr(y, x, str)
int y;
int x;
char *str;

int mvwgetstr(win, y, x, str)
WINDOW *win;
int y;
int x;
char *str;
```

DESCRIPTION

wgetstr() makes a series of calls to wgetch() until a new-line, carriage return, or the Enter key is received. The resulting input string is placed into the reserved area pointed to by str which is assumed to be big enough to contain the resultant input string. If echo is turned on, characters are added to the window win (see echo()). If not in raw() mode, the program is temporarily placed into *cbreak()* mode and the *erase* and *kill* characters are interpreted.

NOTE

functions getstr(), mvgetstr() and mvwgetstr() are pseudo-functions defined in <curses.h>. Also, getstr() and mvgetstr() are specifically set up for use with stdscr.

RETURNS

wgetstr() returns ERR if wgetch() returns ERR (see wgetch()). Otherwise OK is returned.

SEE ALSO

intro, wgetch(), echo(), raw(), cbreak()

[getstr]

NAME

getsyx, setsyx — Get/set the current screen coordinates.

SYNOPSIS

```
#include <curses.h>

void getsyx(y, x)
int y;
int x;

void setsyx(y, x)
int y;
int x;
```

DESCRIPTION

These two routines are designed to be used together by a user-defined function which manipulates *curses* windows but wants the position of the cursor to remain the same. Such a function would call getsyx() to obtain the current cursor coordinates, continue processing the windows, call wnoutrefresh() on each window manipulated, call setsyx() to reset the current cursor coordinates to where they were originally, followed by a call to doupdate().

getsyx() is a pseudo-function defined in the <curses.h> file. It retrieves the current screen coordinates of the virtual screen cursor. These coordinates are where the cursor was placed after the last call to wnoutrefresh(), pnoutrefresh(), wrefresh() or setsyx(), and are placed into the passed arguments y,x. This routine was designed to use the same semantics as other similar routines such as getyx() and setsyx(). The macro prepends each argument with the C-language '&' operator so that the address of each argument is passed. This way, the values of the coordinates can be stored in the passed argument variables.

setsyx() sets the current virtual screen cursor to the values y,x. Note that if leaveok() was TRUE for the last window that was refreshed, then y,x are set to −1,−1. This tells setsyx() to set leaveok().

RETURNS

Void — No return value.

[getsyx]

NOTE
> These routines were introduced with the release of System V.3.

SEE ALSO
> getyx(), leaveok()

NAME
>   getyx, getbegyx, getmaxyx — Obtain current cursor position,
>   window position and window size.

SYNOPSIS
```
#include <curses.h>

getyx(win,y,x)
WINDOW *win;
int y;
int x;

getbegyx(win,y,x)
WINDOW *win;
int y;
int x;

getmaxyx(win,y,x)
WINDOW *win;
int y;
int x;
```

DESCRIPTION
>   getyx() places, in its parameters y and x, the current y,x coordinates
>   of the cursor in the window pointed to by win.
>   Like getyx(), getbegyx() places in its parameters y and x the
>   window's top-left-hand-corner coordinates relative to 0,0 of stdscr.
>   getmaxyx() is used similarly to obtain the window's bottom-right-
>   hand-corner coordinates.

NOTE
>   All these functions are pseudo-functions defined in <curses.h>.
>
>   The pseudo-functions getbegyx() and getmaxyx() were introduced
>   with the release of System V.3.

SEE ALSO
>   getsyx()

[getyx]

NAME
halfdelay — Keyboard input timeout.

SYNOPSIS
```
void halfdelay(tenths)
int tenths;
```

DESCRIPTION
halfdelay() sets up a timeout in tenths of a second. This function is similar to cbreak() in that it sets up the terminal driver to make characters available to the program immediately they are typed at the keyboard. However, halfdelay() introduces a delay time by which wgetch() will block for the time specified. If no characters were typed during this time then wgetch() will return −1. The value of tenths must be between 1 and 255.

To turn halfdelay() off use nocbreak().

RETURNS
Void — No return value.

NOTE
This function was introduced with the release of UNIX System V.

SEE ALSO
cbreak(), wgetch()

[halfdelay]

NAME

idlok — Enable insert/delete-line terminal capability.

SYNOPSIS

```
#include <curses.h>

void idlok(win,boolf)
WINDOW *win;
bool boolf;
```

DESCRIPTION

If the terminal is capable of using the insert/delete-line feature and boolf is TRUE, idlok() will enable this mode. By default *curses* sets boolf to FALSE. *Curses* rarely uses this feature; the insert/delete-character feature is considered first.

If this feature cannot be initiated then *curses* will redraw the changed portions of all lines when refreshed.

RETURNS

Void — No return value.

CAVEAT

This feature should not be used unless you require it (e.g., for an editor program) as it tends to be visually annoying.

While the original intent of this function was to speed up processing it has proved to be inherently slow and visually unpleasant.

[idlok]

NAME
    inch, winch — Get the current character.

SYNOPSIS
    #include <curses.h>

    inch()

    winch(win)
    WINDOW *win;

    int mvinch(y, x)
    int y;
    int x;

    int mvwinch(win, y, x)
    WINDOW *win;
    int y;
    int x;

DESCRIPTION
    winch() returns the character at the current y,x coordinates on the
    window pointed to by win. The character returned will contain all
    attributes (if set for that character position) OR'ed into it.

NOTE
    functions inch(), mvinch() and mvwinch() are pseudo-functions
    defined in <curses.h>. Also inch() and mvinch() are specifically
    set up for use with stdscr.

SEE ALSO
    insch(), getyx()

[inch]

NAME

init_color — Change the definition of a color.

SYNOPSIS

```
#include <curses.h>

int init_color(color, red, green, blue)
int color;
short red;
short green;
short blue;
```

DESCRIPTION

This routine is used to change the definition of a color. The routine does not require a refresh() as the color definition change is immediate, and all occurrences of the color are changed to the new defined color.

The routine takes four arguments: the number of the color to be redefined, and the new values of the red, green and blue components of the color.

The value of color must be between 0 and COLORS −1. The default colors are defined in the <curses.h> file and are as follows:

```
COLOR_BLACK    0
COLOR_BLUE     1
COLOR_GREEN    2
COLOR_CYAN     3
COLOR_RED      4
COLOR_MAGENTA  5
COLOR_YELLOW   6
COLOR_WHITE    7
```

The color with a value of 0 (zero) is assumed to be the default background color for all terminals.

The global variable COLORS defined in <curses.h> is initialized by the function start_color().

The values of red, green and blue must each fall between 0 and 1000.

RETURNS

init_color() returns OK if the color change was possible. Otherwise ERR is returned.

[init_color]

NOTE
>   This function was introduced with the release of System V.3.2.

SEE ALSO
>   `environ()`, `start_color()`, `init_pair()`, `color_content()`,
>   `pair_content()`

[init_color]

NAME

init_pair — Change the definition of a color-pair.

SYNOPSIS

```
#include <curses.h>

int init_pair(colorpair, foreground, background)
int colorpair;
short foreground;
short background;
```

DESCRIPTION

This routine is used to change the definition of a color-pair. The routine does not require a `refresh()` as the color-pair redefinition change is immediate, and all occurrences of the color-pair are changed to the newly defined color-pair.

The routine takes three arguments: the number of the `colorpair` to be redefined, and the new values of the `foreground` and background colors.

The value of `colorpair` must be between 1 and `COLOR_PAIRS` −1. The values of `foreground` and `background` must be between 0 and `COLORS` −1.

The two global variables `COLORS` and `COLOR_PAIRS` are initialized by the function `start_color()`.

RETURNS

init_pair() returns `OK` if the color-pair redefinition was possible. Otherwise `ERR` is returned.

NOTE

This function was introduced with the release of System V.3.2.

SEE ALSO

environ(), start_color(), init_color(), color_content(), pair_content()

[init_pair]

NAME

initscr — *Curses* initialization and start-up routine.

SYNOPSIS

```
#include <curses.h>

WINDOW *initscr()
```

DESCRIPTION

initscr() is used to initialize a *curses* program. The first thing initscr() does is try to figure out what type of terminal it is running on. It does this using the environment variable **TERM**. It then tries to allocate space for the two windows curscr and stdscr, and initializes them and other variables such as LINES, COLS and ttytype. initscr() then sets the terminal into an in-*curses* mode. Finally, initscr() arranges for the terminal screen to be cleared on the first call to wrefresh().

initscr() should be called only once in your program and it must *always* be the first *curses* function called (if you are using windows).

Since this function sets the terminal into an in-*curses* mode, it is not a good idea to issue a call to this routine until you really have to. For example, you may want to do some command line processing first in your program, which often entails printing an error message of some form to stderr.

RETURNS

If an error occurs during the execution of initscr(), then *curses* will call exit() and print an error message to *stderr*. Otherwise a pointer to stdscr is returned.

In termcap versions of *curses*, ERR is returned if any of the following occurs: if initscr() is unable to allocate space for the curscr and stdscr windows; if it is unable to find the environment variable **TERM**; or if it was unable to find an entry for the terminal in the /etc/termcap database.

FILES

/etc/termcap
/usr/lib/terminfo/?

SEE ALSO

setupterm(), longname()

[initscr]

NAME

insch, winsch — Insert a character.

SYNOPSIS

```
#include <curses.h>

int insch(ch)
chtype ch;

int winsch(win,ch)
WINDOW *win;
chtype ch;

int mvinsch(y, x, ch)
int y;
int x;
chtype ch;

int mvwinsch(win, y, x, ch)
WINDOW *win;
int y;
int x;
chtype ch;
```

DESCRIPTION

winsch() inserts the character ch at the current y,x coordinates on the window pointed to by win. Each character after it, is shifted right one place, making the last character on the current line disappear. The current y,x coordinates remain unchanged.

RETURNS

ERR is returned if inserting the character would scroll the screen illegally. Otherwise OK is returned.

NOTE

functions insch(), mvinsch() and mvwinsch() are pseudo-functions defined in <curses.h>. Also, insch() and mvinsch() are specifically set up for use with stdscr.

SEE ALSO

inch()

NAME

insertln, winsertln — Insert a line above the current one.

SYNOPSIS

```
#include <curses.h>

int insertln()

int winsertln(win)
WINDOW *win;
```

DESCRIPTION

winsertln() opens up an empty new line above the current one on the window pointed to by win. Each line below the current line is shifted down by one, and the bottom line of the window is deleted. The current y,x coordinates remain unchanged.

RETURNS

ERR is returned if inserting a new line would scroll the screen illegally. Otherwise OK is returned.

NOTE

The function insertln() is a pseudo-function set up for use with stdscr and is defined in the curses.h file.

NAME

intrflush — Flush keyboard input queue on interrupt.

SYNOPSIS

```
#include <curses.h>

void intrflush(win, boolf)
WINDOW *win;
bool boolf;
```

DESCRIPTION

If the argument boolf is specified as TRUE, then this function will cause the keyboard input queue to be flushed on receipt of a keyboard interrupt (quit or DEL, for example). This enables *curses* to respond to interrupts more quickly, but causes *curses* to have the wrong idea about what is really being displayed on the physical screen. The default for this option is inherited from the terminal driver settings.

If boolf = FALSE, then flushing on interrupts is disabled.

RETURNS

Void — No return value.

NOTE

The parameter win is ignored by this function.

This function does not work on Version 7 UNIX and some Berkeley Systems, as it is essentially a no-op instruction.

This function was introduced with the release of System V.

NAME

keypad — Enable/disable the terminal function key pad.

SYNOPSIS

```
#include <curses.h>

void keypad(win,boolf)
WINDOW *win;
bool boolf;
```

DESCRIPTION

This function allows the programmer to toggle the function key pad on
or off. If enabled (boolf = TRUE), and if a function key (or other
special key such as an arrow key) is depressed, wgetch() treats the
function key specially by returning a token value representation of it. If
disabled (boolf = FALSE), then *curses* does not treat function keys
specially, and leaves the program to interpret the sequence of
characters generated by the function key itself.

If the terminal's keypad is programmable — that is, if it can be
made to transmit when turned on or made to work locally when turned
off — then the keypad is manipulated from within wgetch() when it is
called.

RETURNS

Void — No return value.

NOTE

This function was introduced with the release of System V.

SEE ALSO

wgetch()

[keypad]

NAME

leaveok — Leave cursor at the current location after a change.

SYNOPSIS

```
#include <curses.h>

void leaveok(win, boolf)
WINDOW *win;
bool boolf
```

DESCRIPTION

Normally, when a window is refreshed, the cursor is left at the last character position that was updated on the screen. However, this function allows you to tell *curses* to leave the cursor at the position it originally held on the screen before the refresh took place.

If `boolf` is TRUE, `leaveok()` sets the boolean flag for leaving the cursor where it was last placed, after the window `win` is refreshed. If possible, the cursor is made invisible when this option is enabled.

RETURNS

Void — No return value.

NOTE

Pre-System V versions of *curses* and current Berkeley Distributions implemented this routine as a pseudo-function defined in `<curses.h>`.

NAME

meta — Turn on/off 8-bit input processing.

SYNOPSIS

```
#include <curses.h>

int meta(win, boolf)
WINDOW *win;
bool boolf;
```

DESCRIPTION

If `boolf` is TRUE then characters returned by `wgetch()` for window win are transmitted with all 8 bits, instead of 7 bits (by-default characters are stripped of the highest bit). If `boolf` is FALSE then normal 7-bit processing is resumed.

RETURNS

`meta` returns ERR if it cannot initiate 8-bit processing (probably because `has_meta_key` is not defined in the terminal's terminfo entry); otherwise OK is returned.

NOTE

If any processing is done between the terminal and the program, that strips the eighth bit (networking protocols, for example) then 8-bit processing is impossible.

This function was introduced with the release of System V.

NAME

move, wmove — Change the current y,x coordinates.

SYNOPSIS

```
#include <curses.h>

int move(y,x)
int y;
int x;

int wmove(win,y,x)
WINDOW *win;
int y;
int x;
```

DESCRIPTION

wmove() changes the current y,x coordinates of the window pointed to by win to the new coordinates specified by y and x.

RETURNS

ERR if the new coordinates exceed the maximum dimensions of the window. Otherwise OK is returned and the new coordinates are set.

NOTE

The function move() is a pseudo-function set up for use with stdscr and is defined in the curses.h file.

NAME
mvcur — Low-level cursor motion.

SYNOPSIS

```
void mvcur(oldline, oldcol, newline, newcol)
int oldline;
int oldcol;
int newline;
int newcol;
```

DESCRIPTION
This routine uses the current cursor coordinates `oldline`, `newline` and the new required cursor coordinates `newline`, `newcol`, to move the cursor to the newly desired location. It does this very efficiently by calculating the total cost of moving the cursor from where it is to where it is going. Several strategies are considered, depending on what the terminal is capable of. For example, there may be fewer characters generated by using local (up, down, left, right) cursor motion than by using the absolute cursor-addressing capability.

It is possible to use this function without using the other *curses* functions. However, so that the *curses* routines know what is going on, it is recommended that you use `move()` followed by `refresh()` instead.

RETURNS
Void — No return value.

SEE ALSO
`move(), refresh()`

[mvcur]

NAME

mvwin — Move the window to a new location.

SYNOPSIS

```
#include <curses.h>

int mvwin(win, y, x)
WINDOW *win;
int y;
int x;
```

DESCRIPTION

This function relocates the window `win` so that the upper left-hand corner of the window is placed at the new position on the screen specified by the arguments y,x, where y corresponds to the new line offset, and x corresponds to the new column offset.

RETURNS

`mvwin()` returns ERR if the new locations would move any portion of the window off the edge of the screen. If this is the case, the window is not moved. OK is returned otherwise.

NAME

napms — Put a process to sleep for a specified time in milliseconds.

SYNOPSIS

```
int napms(ms)
int ms;
```

DESCRIPTION

This routine, if supported on your system (it is very system-dependent), puts the current process to sleep for a time specified in milliseconds.

The resolution of ms may not be exact in its execution, because the unit of resolution can vary between systems. Generally, 60ths of a second is the norm; if you want to sleep for any period of time greater than 3/4 of a second you should use the standard sleep(3) system call.

RETURNS

This routine does not exist on some systems and even where it does, it may not work. If this is the case ERR is returned, otherwise OK is returned.

SEE ALSO

delay_output(), draino()

sleep(3) in the UNIX Programmer's Reference Manual

NAME

newpad — Create a new pad.

SYNOPSIS

```
#include <curses.h>

WINDOW *newpad(nlines,ncols)
int nlines;
int ncols;
```

DESCRIPTION

This function is similar to newwin(), but makes a pad instead of a window. A pad is not associated with any part of the screen, so it can be any reasonable size. The arguments nlines and ncols specify the dimensions of the new pad in lines and columns respectively.

Pads are typically used when a window bigger than the physical screen is required.

RETURNS

if newpad() encounters an error, then (WINDOW *)NULL is returned. Otherwise a pointer to the new pad is returned.

NOTE

This function was introduced with the release of UNIX System V.

SEE ALSO

newwin(), prefresh(), pnoutrefresh(), subpad()

NAME

newterm, set_term — Alternative *curses* initialization functions.

SYNOPSIS

```
#include <curses.h>

SCREEN *newterm(nterm, outfp, infp)
char *nterm;
FILE *outfp;
FILE *infp;

SCREEN *set_term(new)
SCREEN *new;
```

DESCRIPTION

If your *curses* program needs to manage more than one terminal, then newterm() should be used in place of initscr(). newterm() should be called once for each terminal that your program will use. The pointer returned points to a SCREEN structure which is internally set up to reflect the type of terminal (specified in nterm) that you want to manipulate. The arguments outfp and infp are UNIX stdio type FILE pointers and are used for the terminal's output and input. For example, the function initscr() calls:

```
newterm(getenv("TERM"), stdout, stdin).
```

The pointer returned from newterm() should be saved as a reference to the specified terminal. It is then possible to switch between different terminal environments by using the pointer as an argument to set_term(). The function set_term() is the only routine within the library which uses SCREEN pointers, and it returns a pointer to the previous SCREEN.

The SCREEN structure format is hidden from the user, mainly to keep the *curses* library portable, as this structure tends to change with each new update of the *curses* package. The definition for it is in <curses.h> and is referenced as an extern. The structure contains the complete *curses* working environment for the terminal being used, including the TERMINAL structure containing the terminal's capabilities as obtained from the terminfo database.

Note that before a program exits, it must call endwin() for each terminal being used.

[newterm]

RETURNS

newterm() returns (SCREEN *)NULL if it could not allocate enough memory. Otherwise a pointer to the new SCREEN structure is returned.

set_term() returns a pointer to the previous set-up SCREEN.

NOTE

These functions were introduced with the release of UNIX System V.

SEE ALSO

setupterm(), set_curterm(), initscr(), endwin()

stdio(3S), getenv(3C) in the UNIX System V Programmer's Reference Manual

[newterm]

NAME

newwin — Create a new window.

SYNOPSIS

```
#include <curses.h>

WINDOW *newwin(nlines,ncols,begy,begx)
int nlines;
int ncols;
int begy;
int begx;
```

DESCRIPTION

This routine creates a new *curses* window whose dimensions are
specified in the parameters as follows: the number of lines in the new
window (nlines); the number of columns in the new window (ncols);
which line with relation to 0 of stdscr the window will start from
(begy); and which column with relation to 0 of stdscr the window will
start from (begx).

The upper left corner of the new window is placed at y = begy
and x = begx. If either of nlines or ncols is 0, then newwin() will
default their values to (lines - begy) and (cols - begx).
Consequently, the call newwin(0,0,0,0) creates a full screen window.

RETURNS

newwin() returns (WINDOW *)NULL if either begy or begx are less
than zero or if memory cannot be allocated for the new window.
Otherwise a pointer to the new window is returned.

[newwin]

NAME
nl, nonl — Toggle on/off new-line mode.

SYNOPSIS

```
void nl()

void nonl()
```

DESCRIPTION
These routines set (nl()) or unset (nonl()) the terminal *tty* driver so that the system either continues or stops mapping RETURN to NEWLINE on output.

If mapping is disabled with nonl(), then wrefresh() can do more optimization by making better use of the line-feed capability; this will result in faster cursor motion.

RETURNS
Void — No return value.

NOTE
Pre-System V versions of *curses* and current Berkeley Distributions implemented these routines as pseudo-functions defined in <curses.h>

[nl]

NAME

nodelay — Toggle input delay on/off.

SYNOPSIS

```
#include <curses.h>

void nodelay(win, boolf)
WINDOW *win;
bool boolf;
```

DESCRIPTION

This routine manipulates the *tty* driver to turn on (`boolf` = `TRUE`) or off (`boolf` = `FALSE`) NODELAY mode. If `boolf` is `TRUE`, then nodelay() will cause wgetch() to return immediately with `ERR` if no character is waiting in the input queue. If `boolf` is `FALSE`, wgetch() will hang until a key is pressed on the keyboard.

RETURNS

Void — No return value.

NOTE

Version 7 UNIX and Berkeley do not provide kernel support for this mode, so the function does not exist on these systems.

SEE ALSO

`termio(7)` in the UNIX System V Programmer's Reference Manual

[nodelay]

NAME

notimeout — Toggle internal input timer.

SYNOPSIS

```
#include <curses.h>

void notimeout(win, boolf)
WINDOW *win;
bool boolf;
```

DESCRIPTION

If `boolf` is TRUE, the internal timer is not set. This prevents `wgetch()` from treating the *escape* character specially.

The default is `boolf` = FALSE. This causes `wgetch()` to wait for a short period (after receiving an escape character) to see if any other characters are received. Eventually (if no other characters are received during this period) `wgetch()` will timeout and return the *escape* character to the caller. This is so that `wgetch()` can tell the difference between an escape sequence from, say, a function key, or detect that the user has just pressed the escape key.

If a function or keypad key is depressed and `boolf` = FALSE the program may seem to pause for a while, depending on the length of the escape sequence produced by the key. Also, `wgetch()` will return a token value representing whatever key was depressed.

RETURNS

Void — No return value.

NOTE

This function was introduced with the release of System V.3.

SEE ALSO

`wgetch()`

NAME

overlay — Overlay a window on top of another, non-destructively.

SYNOPSIS

```
#include <curses.h>

int overlay(win1,win2)
WINDOW *win1;
WINDOW *win2;
```

DESCRIPTION

The contents of the window pointed to by win1 are copied onto the window pointed to by win2, insofar as they fit, starting from their y=0, x=0 coordinates. This is done **non-destructively**; in other words, blanks on win1 leave the contents of the space on win2 untouched.

RETURNS

System V.3 returns ERR if win2 will not fit within the bounds of win1, or else OK is returned. Pre-System V.3 versions of this function have no return value.

SEE ALSO

overwrite(), copywin()

[overlay]

NAME

overwrite — Overlay a window on top of another, destructively.

SYNOPSIS

```
#include <curses.h>

int overwrite(win1,win2)
WINDOW *win1;
WINDOW *win2;
```

DESCRIPTION

The contents of the window pointed to by win1 are copied onto the window pointed to by win2, insofar as they fit, starting from their y=0, x=0 coordinates. This is done **destructively**; in other words, blanks on win1 become blanks on win2.

RETURNS

System V.3 returns ERR if win2 will not fit within the bounds of win1, or else OK is returned. Pre-System V.3 versions of this function have no return value.

SEE ALSO

overlay(), copywin()

NAME
pair_content — Obtain color-pair content information.

SYNOPSIS
```
#include <curses.h>

int pair_content(colorpair, foreground, background)
int colorpair;
short *foreground;
short *background;
```

DESCRIPTION
This routine is used to determine what the colors of a given color-pair consist of.

The routine uses three arguments: the colorpair number which must be a value between 1 and COLOR_PAIRS −1, and the addresses of two shorts for storing the obtained color components of foreground and background. The function will store the current values at these addresses passed. The values will be between 0 (zero) and COLORS −1.

The global variables COLORS and COLOR_PAIRS are defined in the <curses.h> file and are initialized by the function start_color().

RETURNS
pair_content() returns ERR if the color-pair was not initialized. Otherwise OK is returned.

NOTE
This function was introduced with the release of System V.3.2.

SEE ALSO
environ(),   start_color(),   init_pair(),   init_color(), color_content()

[pair_content]

NAME

prefresh — Update *(refresh)* a pad on the screen.

SYNOPSIS

```
#include <curses.h>

int prefresh(pad, pminrow, pmincol, sminrow,
             smincol, smaxrow, smaxcol)

int pnoutrefresh(pad, pminrow, pmincol, sminrow,
             smincol, smaxrow, smaxcol)
WINDOW *pad;
int pminrow;
int pmincol;
int sminrow;
int smincol;
int smaxrow;
int smaxcol;
```

DESCRIPTION

These functions are similar to `wrefresh()` and `wnoutrefresh()` except that they operate on a pad instead of a window. A pad is not necessarily associated with any particular part of the terminal screen and (unlike a window) it can be of any reasonable size. Therefore the additional parameters are needed to specify which part of the pad is to be updated and on what part of the physical screen it is to be displayed.

The parameters `pminrow` and `pmincol` are the upper left-hand corners of the rectangle within the pad which will be put on the screen. However, the specified rectangle may be too big to fit on the screen, so the parameters `sminrow`, `smincol`, `smaxrow` and `smaxcol` are used to specify which rectangular portion of the physical screen will be affected. Arguments `sminrow` and `smincol` are the upper left-hand corner of the screen, and `smaxrow` and `smaxcol` are the lower right-hand corner. From this information, these functions are able to calculate the size of the rectangular portion of the pad which is to be updated.

`pnoutrefresh()` updates the `curses` virtual screen `curscr` with the contents of the rectangular portion of the pad to be displayed. No actual update is done to the physical screen, whereas the function `prefresh()` calls `pnoutrefresh()` then `doupdate()` which updates the physical screen.

[prefresh]

RETURNS

pnoutrefresh() returns ERR if pad is NULL or sminrow is greater than smaxrow or smincol is greater than smaxcol. Otherwise OK is returned.

prefresh() returns the number of characters transmitted to the physical terminal screen.

NOTE

These functions were introduced with the release of UNIX System V.

SEE ALSO

wrefresh(), wnoutrefresh(), doupdate()

[prefresh]

NAME

printw, wprintw — Print formatted output to a window.

SYNOPSIS

```
#include <curses.h>

int printw(fmt [,arg]...)
char *fmt;

int wprintw(win,fmt [,arg]...)
WINDOW *win;
char *fmt;

int mvprintw(y, x, fmt, [,arg]...)
int y;
int x;
char *fmt;

int mvwprintw(win, y, x, fmt, [,arg]...)
WINDOW *win;
int y;
int x;
char *fmt;


#include <varargs.h>

int vwprintw(win, fmt, varglist)
WINDOW *win;
char *fmt;
va_list varglist;
```

DESCRIPTION

These functions implement a printf(3) on a window. Unlike other similar functions which use macros for their prefixed versions, these are built-in *curses* functions, due to the variable number of arguments used. However, the functions printw() and mvprintw() are specifically set up for use with stdscr.

The functions wprintw() and mvwprintw() use the window pointed to by win. The arguments y,x specify the location to print the string within the specified window.

Each of these functions converts, formats and prints its arguments arg on the window, under control of the format argument fmt.

[printw]

These functions actually use the `stdio(3S)` package to construct the string from the specified format.   `fmt` is a character string and may contain either printable characters or conversion specifications, as with the `printf(3S)` function.

Routines such as these are inherently non-portable because argument-passing conventions often differ between machines. For this reason the variable argument list system was introduced with UNIX System V. The system is implemented by using a set of macros which allow portable variable argument lists to be written. The function `vwprintw()` uses this system. It is functionally the same as `wprintw()` except that the last argument `varglist` is a pointer to a list of arguments as defined in the `<varargs.h>` include file.

RETURNS

`ERR` is returned if adding the string to the window would scroll the screen illegally. Otherwise `OK` is returned.

NOTE

The function `vwprintw()` was introduced with the release of UNIX System V.3.

SEE ALSO

`stdio(3S)`, `printf(3S)` and `varargs(5)` in the UNIX System V Programmer's Reference Manual

[printw]

NAME
raw, noraw — Toggle raw mode on/off.

SYNOPSIS

```
void raw()
```

```
void noraw()
```

DESCRIPTION
These functions set (`raw()`) or unset (`noraw()`) the terminal *tty* driver *into* or *out-of* raw mode.

Raw mode is similar to `cbreak()` mode in that characters typed are immediately made available to the program as they are typed at the keyboard. However, in raw mode the *interrupt, quit* and *control-flow* input control characters are uninterpreted by the driver instead of generating a signal (default). The DEL or BREAK keys for the purposes of raw mode remain the same and are not manipulated within *curses* (see `signal(2)`).

RETURNS
Void — No return value.

NOTE
Pre-System V versions of *curses* and current Berkeley Distributions implemented these routines as pseudo-functions defined in `<curses.h>`

On Version 7 UNIX systems these routines also turn off new-line mapping.

SEE ALSO
`cbreak(), crmode()`

`signal(2), termio(7)` in the UNIX System V Programmer's Reference Manual

[raw]

NAME

refresh, wrefresh — Update the terminal screen.

SYNOPSIS

```
#include <curses.h>

int refresh()

int wrefresh(win)
WINDOW *win;
```

DESCRIPTION

wrefresh() synchronizes the curscr window with the window pointed to by win, and in effect overlays the contents of the window on the terminal screen. If the window is not a screen, only that part covered by it is updated.

The function calls wnoutrefresh() to initiate the update. Then doupdate() is called to perform the update.

RETURNS

ERR if it would scroll the screen illegally; if this is the case, the screen is updated, but the lower right-hand corner of the terminal screen is not written to. If no errors are found, OK is returned.

NOTE

The function refresh() is a pseudo-function set up for use with stdscr and is defined in the curses.h file.

SEE ALSO

wnoutrefresh(), doupdate()

[refresh]

NAME

reset_prog_mode, reset_shell_mode — Reset current terminal modes.

SYNOPSIS

```
void reset_prog_mode()

void reset_shell_mode()
```

DESCRIPTION

These routines restore the terminal to modes previously saved with the functions `def_prog_mode()` and `def_shell_mode()`.

The function `reset_prog_mode()` sets the terminal into an in-*curses* state, while the function `reset_shell_mode()` sets the terminal into an out-of-*curses* state. Note that this is done automatically by `endwin()` and `doupdate()`.

RETURNS

Void — No return value.

NOTE

These functions were introduced with the release of System V and replaced the functions `resetterm()` and `fixterm()` of earlier releases.

SEE ALSO

`def_prog_mode()`, `def_shell_mode()`, `savetty()`, `resetty()`, `initscr()`, `setupterm()`

`termio(7)` in the UNIX System V Programmer's Reference Manual

NAME

restartterm — Re-initialize *curses* environment after a memory save/restore.

SYNOPSIS

```
void restartterm(term, fildes, errret)
char *term;
int fildes;
int *errret;
```

DESCRIPTION

This function is similar to `setupterm()` except that space is not allocated for a new `TERMINAL` structure internally. The function is called after restoring memory from a previous state, usually after a call to `scr_restore()`. It assumes that the terminal's driver modes are set to what they were when memory was saved, but the terminal type and baud rate may have changed.

The argument `term` specifies the terminal type you want to re-initialize. If `term` is a NULL pointer, then `restartterm()` does a `getenv("TERM")` internally. The argument `fildes` is not a stdio `FILE` pointer but a UNIX file descriptor. This descriptor is an open file handle (returned from the system call `open(2)`) which is used for output. Normally this is the `stdout` channel, specified as 1.

The pointer `errret` points to an integer which is used to store the return condition if an error occurs (see NOTE below). If this is specified as `(int *)0`, then errors are handled internally and a message acknowledging the error is printed; the function then calls `exit(2)`. If `errret` is not NULL then the stored value is either 0 (meaning the terminfo description for the terminal `term` was not available) or −1 (which means the terminfo database could not be found). Usually you call `restartterm((char *)0, 1, (int *)0)`.

RETURNS

Void — No return value.

NOTE

The UNIX System V.3 version of this function ignores the argument `errret` and errors are handled internally.

This function was introduced with the release of UNIX System V.

SEE ALSO

`setupterm()`, `scr_retore()`, `scr_init()`

`getenv(3C)`, `stdio(3S)`, `open(2)`, `exit(2)` in the UNIX System V Programmer's Reference Manual

[restartterm]

NAME

ripoffline — Reduce the size of the screen by one line.

SYNOPSIS

```
void ripoffline(line, init_func)
int line;
int (*init_func)();
```

DESCRIPTION

This function allows you to rip off a single line from the stdscr window. The function slk_init() does this internally, but ripoffline() allows you to access the same facility without initializing screen labels. Up to 5 lines can be ripped off the screen by calling ripoffline() consecutively.

The argument line is an arbitrary number which merely indicates where the line is to be stripped off. If line is positive the line is stripped off the top of the screen; if it is negative it is stripped off the bottom. ripoffline() must be called before initscr() or newterm() so that they can arrange for the screen size to be reduced.

The supplied initialization function init_func() is called from within initscr() or newterm() if ripoffline() has been called. This function is supplied with two arguments: a pointer to a one-line window, and the width of the window in columns. The global variables LINES and COLS are not guaranteed to be correct inside init_func(), therefore wrefresh() and doupdate() must not be called.

RETURNS

Void — No return value.

NOTE

Although the UNIX System V Programmer's Reference Manual specifies that it is allowable to call wnoutrefresh() from within the supplied function, on some systems this causes a *core dump*. It is therefore recommended that wnoutrefresh() is called on the passed window pointer after calling initscr() or newterm(). This can be done by saving the passed window pointer using a global pointer defined in your source file.

This function was introduced with the release of UNIX System V.3.

SEE ALSO

slk_init()

[ripoffline]

NAME

savetty, resetty — Save/restore terminal driver modes.

SYNOPSIS

```
void savetty()

void resetty()
```

DESCRIPTION

These routines save (savetty()) and restore (resetty()) the state of the terminal driver modes. savetty() stores the current state of the terminal in an internal buffer and resetty() restores the state of the terminal to that which was saved by savetty().

RETURNS

Void — No return value.

SEE ALSO

```
setupterm(),       def_prog_mode(),       def_shell_mode(),
reset_prog_mode(), reset_shell_mode()
```

[savetty]

NAME
scanw, wscanw — Formatted read from a window.

SYNOPSIS
```
#include <curses.h>

int scanw(fmt, [,arg]...)
char *fmt;

int wscanw(win, fmt, [,arg]...)
WINDOW *win;
char *fmt;

int mvscanw(y, x, fmt, [,arg]...)
int y;
int x;
char *fmt;

int mvwscanw(win, y, x, fmt, [,arg]...)
WINDOW *win;
int y;
int x;
char *fmt;


#include <varargs.h>

int vwscanw(win, fmt, varglist)
WINDOW *win;
char *fmt;
va_list varglist;
```

DESCRIPTION
These functions implement a scanf(3S) on a window. Unlike other similar functions which use macros for their prefixed versions, these are built-in *curses* functions, due to the variable number of arguments used. However, the functions scanw() and mvscanw() are specifically set up for use with stdscr.

Each function reads characters from the specified window win (stdscr in the case of scanw or mvscanw), interprets them according to the format fmt, then stores the results in its arguments. The string is then added to the window at the current y,x locations unless, of course, the move versions are used.

[scanw]

Routines such as these are inherently non-portable because argument-passing conventions often differ between machines. For this reason the variable argument list system was introduced with UNIX System V. The system is implemented by using a set of macros which allow portable variable argument lists to be written. The function `vwscanw()` uses this system. It is functionally the same as `wscanw()` except that the last argument `varglist` is a pointer to a list of arguments as defined in the `<varargs.h>` include file.

RETURNS

The number of characters read are returned.

NOTE

The function `vwscanw()` was introduced with the release of UNIX System V.3.

SEE ALSO

`scanf(3S)` and `varargs(5)` in the UNIX System V Programmer's Reference Manual

NAME

scr_dump, scr_restore, scr_init — Save/restore/share *curses* virtual screen image.

SYNOPSIS

```
int scr_dump(filename)
char *filename;

int scr_restore(filename)
char *filename;

int scr_init(filename)
char *filename;
```

DESCRIPTION

The function scr_dump() dumps a copy of the virtual screen (curscr) to the file filename. The function scr_retore() can then be used to restore the current virtual screen to what was saved by scr_dump(). When this function is called, all current data on the screen is lost — unless, of course, a previous scr_dump() was issued beforehand, in which case the previous screen data can be restored by a subsequent call to scr_restore().

The argument filename specifies the name of the file to save/restore the screen dump to/from. This is overwritten by each subsequent call to scr_dump(), using the same file name.

The next call to doupdate() will activate the restore and re-establish the screen to how it was before the dump.

The file format of the dump file is as follows (although this may change in subsequent releases of System V). Generally, the MAGIC number stored in the dump file must be the same as the MAGIC number which the current version of *curses* is expecting.

```
[magic number]
[name of tty, 20 characters]
[modification time of tty, type time_t]
[columns]
[lines]
[line 1 length] [string of chars in line]
[line 2 length] [string of chars in line]
   . . .
   . . .
[line n length] [string of chars in line]
[labels flag]
```

[scr_dump]

[number of labels, if labels flag set]
[label 1, if labels flag set]
[label 2, if labels flag set]

. . .

. . .

[label n, if labels flag set]
[Y coordinate of cursor]
[X coordinate of cursor]

In the case of `scr_init()`, the contents of the dump are read in and used to fix up the internal *curses* data structures so that they reflect what the terminal is now displaying. Provided that the data read in is valid, *curses* will base its next screen update on the information obtained rather than clearing, redrawing and starting from scratch.

`scr_init()` has been specifically designed so that screen dumps can be shared by more than one process. To do this, the function makes sure that the process which created the dump is in sync with what the current terminal is displaying. It assumes that if the modification time of the terminal is not the same as that specified in the dump file, the screen image on that terminal has changed from what is in the dump, and the latter is now invalid. Both processes must be run from the same terminal.

Typically a process would use `system(3S)` to start up another process. The second process creates the dump file and exits without causing the terminal's time stamp to change. It does this by calling `endwin()` followed by `scr_dump()` and then `exit()`. Control is passed back to the first process, which calls `scr_int()` to update its screen contents so that it reflects what is specified in the dump file.

RETURNS

`scr_dump()` returns ERR if the argument `filename` cannot be opened for writing.

`scr_restore()` and `scr_init()` return ERR if `filename` cannot be opened for reading, or if the magic number is invalid.

`scr_init()` returns ERR if the time stamp of the dump file is old, or the capability `nrrmc` is TRUE. Therefore programs should not call `putp(exit_ca_mode)` before calling `scr_init()`.

OK is returned from all functions otherwise.

NOTE

These routines were introduced with the release of System V.3.

[scr_dump]

SEE ALSO

> endwin(), restartterm()

> types(5) in the UNIX System V Programmer's Reference Manual

NAME
>
> scroll — Scroll window up a line.

SYNOPSIS

```
#include <curses.h>

void scroll(win)
WINDOW *win;
```

DESCRIPTION
>
> scroll() scrolls the window up a line. This is done within the specified window's data structure. If the window is a full screen and the scrolling region takes up the whole screen, then as an optimization the scroll is performed by a physical hardware scroll.

RETURNS
>
> Void — No return value.

SEE ALSO

```
scrollok(), setscrreg()
```

[scroll]

NAME

scrollok — Toggle window scrolling.

SYNOPSIS

```
#include <curses.h>

int scrollok(win,boolf)
WINDOW *win;
bool boolf;
```

DESCRIPTION

scrollok() manipulates the scroll/on scroll/off toggle on the specified window win. If boolf is TRUE, the window scrolls up a line if the current line is the bottom line of the window or scrolling region, and a new-line, carriage-return or enter is encountered. If the window is a full screen and the scrolling region takes up the whole screen, then as an optimization the scroll is performed by a physical hardware scroll. In either case a wrefresh() is called on the window. If boolf is FALSE, the cursor is left on the line where the offending character was entered.

RETURNS

scrollok1 returns OK regardless.

NOTE

Pre-System V versions of *curses* and current Berkeley Distributions implemented this routine as a pseudo-function defined in <curses.h>.

SEE ALSO

scroll(), setscrreg()

[scrollok]

NAME

set_curterm — Set the current terminfo environment.

SYNOPSIS

```
#include <term.h>

TERMINAL *set_curterm(nterm)
TERMINAL *nterm;
```

DESCRIPTION

This low-level terminfo function allows a program to switch its terminfo environment to that of another terminal type, thereby allowing a program to manipulate more than one terminal type.

set_curterm() sets the terminfo variable cur_term to point to the passed TERMINAL structure nterm. The new terminfo environment then uses the boolean, numeric and string variables set up in nterm.

The argument nterm points to a TERMINAL structure which is assumed to have been originally filled in by setupterm().

RETURNS

set_curterm() returns a pointer to a TERMINAL structure which represents the previous TERMINAL environment.

If nterm is a NULL pointer the environment is not changed and a pointer to cur_term is returned.

NOTE

This function was introduced with the release of System V.3.

SEE ALSO

del_curterm(), setupterm()

[set_curterm]

NAME

setscrreg, wsetscrreg — Preset scrolling region.

SYNOPSIS

```
#include <curses.h>

setscrreg(top,bot)
int top;
int bot;

wsetscrreg(win,top,bot)
WINDOW *win;
int top;
int bot;
```

DESCRIPTION

These routines are implemented as pseudo-functions defined in
<curses.h>. They make it possible to set a software scrolling region
within the window specified by the argument win. The parameters top
and bot specify the top and bottom margins of the scrolling region
required within the window.

Provided that scrolling is allowed in the window (see scrollok()),
an attempt to move off the bottom line of the scrolling region will
cause all the lines in the window to scroll up a line. If the scrolling
region takes up the whole window and win is a full screen, then as an
optimization the scroll is performed as a physical hardware scroll.

NOTE

The function setscrreg() has been specifically set up for use with
stdscr.

These routines were introduced with the release of System V.2.

SEE ALSO

scroll(), scrollok()

[setscrreg]

NAME

setupterm — Low-level terminfo initialization.

SYNOPSIS

```
#include <term.h>

int setupterm(term, fildes, errret)
char *term;
int fildes;
int *errret;
```

DESCRIPTION

This is the low-level terminfo start-up routine. The argument `term` is usually the resultant character pointer returned by `getenv("TERM")`. This specifies the terminal type you want to work with. If `term` is a NULL pointer, then `setupterm()` does a `getenv("TERM")` internally anyway. The argument `fildes` is not a `stdio FILE` pointer but a UNIX file descriptor. This descriptor (an open file handle) is used for output and is normally specified as 1 (`stdout`). The pointer `errret` points to a locally defined integer which will contain the return condition if an error occurs. However, if this is specified as `(int *)0`, then errors are handled internally and a message acknowledging the error is printed followed by a call to `exit(2)`. If `errret` is not a NULL pointer then the stored value is either 0 (meaning the terminfo description for the terminal specified was not available) or −1 (which means the terminfo database could not be found). Usually you call `setupterm((char *)0, 1, (int *)0)`.

If `setupterm()` does not encounter an error it allocates and sets up a new `TERMINAL` data structure so that it reflects the specified terminal. This structure contains all the information about the terminal including the boolean, numeric and string capabilities. Also, the global variable `ttytype` (an array of characters containing the terminal aliases) is initialized along with other variables to be used by other terminfo routines. The `TERMINAL` pointer `cur_term` is then set to point to this area.

The area reserved by `setupterm()` is not static, therefore each call allocates a new `TERMINAL` structure and the `cur_term` pointer then points to that. If the pointer `cur_term` is saved it will then be possible to switch between `TERMINAL` structures with `set_curterm()`.

[setupterm]

RETURNS

This function returns ERR if an error was encountered. Otherwise OK is returned.

NOTE

This function was introduced with the release of UNIX System V.

SEE ALSO

initscr(), set_curterm(), del_curterm()

getenv(3C), stdio(3S), exit(2), open(2) in the UNIX System V Programmer's Reference Manual

NAME

slk_clear, slk_init, slk_label, slk_noutrefresh, slk_refresh,
slk_restore, slk_set, slk_touch — Routines to manipulate soft
function key labels.

SYNOPSIS

```
void slk_clear();

void slk_init(format)
int format;

char *slk_label(labelnum)
int labelnum;

void slk_noutrefresh();

void slk_refresh();

void slk_restore();

int slk_set(labelnum, label, format)
int labelnum;
char *label;
int format;

void slk_touch();
```

DESCRIPTION

These functions make it possible to program the programmable *soft
labels* often found on some of the more modern terminals. If the
terminal does not support this feature, then *curses* takes over the
bottom line of stdscr, at the same time reducing the size of stdscr
and LINES by one line. *Curses* uses the standard size of a label which
is 8 characters and there are 8 labels across the screen starting from
column 0.

If you want to use soft labels you must issue a call to slk_init()
before calling initscr(). Internally initscr() calls newterm() to
set up the terminal type. If the terminal does not support soft labels,
this function needs to know that the stdscr window is to be 1 line
shorter. Calling slk_init() before newterm() sets up internal
variables to inform newterm() that soft-label programming is desired.
If you issue a direct call to newterm() anywhere within your program
and you intend to program soft labels, you must also make sure that
you issue a call to slk_init() first.

[slk_clear]

If initscr() finds that it must use the bottom line of stdscr, the parameter format specifies the label arrangement on the screen. If format = 0, then the format is arranged in a 3-2-3 arrangement; if format = 1, a 4-4 arrangement is used.

The function slk_set() is used to set up a soft label. labelnum is the number of the label to set up, from 1 to 8. label is a NULL terminated string not more than 8 characters in length which will be put on the label. format is either 0, 1 or 2, specifying that the string to put on the label is to be left-justified, centered, or right-justified respectively. A NULL pointer forces a blank label. If labelnum or format are illegal, ERR is returned; otherwise OK is returned.

The functions slk_refresh() and slk_noutrefresh() are analogous to wrefresh() and wnoutrefresh(). You would normally use slk_noutrefresh() on each label that needs updating and then make a single call to slk_refresh() to instigate the update. This reduces the amount of characters transmitted to the terminal and aids optimization.

slk_label() returns the contents of the current label specified in labelnum.

The functions slk_clear() and slk_restore() allow you to clear and restore the soft label.

slk_touch() forces all soft labels to be updated at the next call to slk_refresh().

NOTE

These functions were introduced with the release of System V.3.

SEE ALSO

doupdate(), ripoffline()

[slk_clear]

NAME

standout, wstandout, standend, wstandend — Start and stop
standout mode.

SYNOPSIS

```
#include <curses.h>

int standout()

int wstandout(win)
WINDOW *win;

int standend()

int wstandend(win)
WINDOW *win;
```

DESCRIPTION

wstandout() and wstandend() set or clear the video attribute
standout, respectively. If this attribute is set, each character added to
the window pointed to by win is OR'ed with A_STANDOUT and will
appear on the terminal screen in standout (often reverse video)
mode.

If the terminal is not capable of displaying in this mode, another
suitable method of displaying is sought from the terminal description
database (underline, for example). Otherwise it displays characters as
they are normally displayed.

By default, standout mode is turned off when a new window is
created. However, sub-windows created with subwin() inherit
attributes set in the parent. This particular attribute can, of course, be
switched off by a subsequent call to wstandend() on the sub-window.

The functions standout() and standend() are pseudo-functions
set up for use with stdscr and are defined in the <curses.h> file.
They are expanded to wstandout(stdscr) and wstandend(stdscr)
respectively by the C preprocessor.

RETURNS

OK is returned regardless.

SEE ALSO

attron(), attroff()

[standout]

NAME
start_color — Initialize and set up *curses* for color mode.

SYNOPSIS

```
int start_color()
```

DESCRIPTION
This routine restores the terminal's colors to the values that were originally set up when the terminal was turned on, and then sets up *curses* for color mode.

Eight basic colors are initialized: black, blue, green, cyan, red, magenta, yellow, and white. Two global variables — COLORS and COLOR_PAIRS, as defined in the <curses.h> header file — are also initialized. These variables define the maximum number of colors and the maximum number of color-pairs supported by the current terminal.

This routine must be called before any other *curses* routine which manipulates or uses color. A good place to call it is immediately after calling initscr().

RETURNS
start_color() returns ERR if the terminal does not support colors. Otherwise OK is returned.

NOTE
This function was introduced with the release of System V.3.2.

SEE ALSO
environ(), init_pair(), init_color(), color_content(), pair_content()

[start_color]

NAME

subwin, subpad — Create a sub-window/subpad.

SYNOPSIS

```
#include <curses.h>

WINDOW *subwin(orig, nlines, ncols, begy, begx)
WINDOW *orig;
int nlines;
int ncols;
int begy;
int begx;

WINDOW *subpad(orig, nlines, ncols, begy, begx)
WINDOW *orig;
int nlines;
int ncols;
int begy;
int begx;
```

DESCRIPTION

These functions create and return a pointer to a new window. The
window returned is adopted by the parent window `orig`, or in the case
of `subpad()`, the parent pad. The arguments `nlines` and `ncols`
specify the dimensions of the new window/pad.

In the case of `subwin()`, the upper left corner of the new window
is placed at `begy,begx` on the screen. This position is in relation to the
screen and not to the parent window `orig`.

In the case of `subpad()`, the window is placed at `begy,begx` on
the pad. Since a pad is not necessarily associated with any part of the
screen, this position may not always fall within the bounds of the
terminal's display.

In either case, the new window/pad is made as if it represents part
of the parent `orig`. In other words, changes to one window will affect
the character image of both windows.

After a sub-window/pad is modified, `touchwin()` or `touchline()`
should be called on `orig` before refreshing it.

NOTE

When refreshing a pad you must use `prefresh()` and not
`wrefresh()`.

The function `subpad()` was introduced with the release of System V.

[subwin]

SEE ALSO

```
wrefresh(), prefresh(), touchwin(), touchline()
```

[subwin]

NAME

tgetent, tgetflag, tgetnum, tgetstr — Low-level *termcap* entry
and query functions.

SYNOPSIS

```
int tgetent(bp, name)
char *bp;
char *name;

int tgetflag(codename)
char *codename;

int tgetnum(codename)
char *codename;

char *tgetstr(codename, area)
char *codename;
char *area;
```

DESCRIPTION

These low-level *termcap* functions are emulated by using the *terminfo*
library.   codename must be a *termcap* two-code string: for example,
"cm" is used for the cursor-addressing capability.

The function tgetent() uses name which is normally the resultant
string returned from getenv("TERM"), to search for the *termcap*
database entry for the terminal in use. It then fills the first 1024 bytes
of the supplied area pointed to by bp with the information found. This
area is then used by the other *termcap* routines. By default the
/etc/termcap file is scanned, but if the shell environment variable
TERMCAP is set, then tgetent() uses this instead. However, because
tgetent() is emulated using terminfo, the argument bp is totally
ignored and none of this is done.

The functions tgetflag(), tgetnum() and tgetstr() return
the boolean entry, the numeric entry, and the string entry respectively.
If the argument area used by tgetstr() is not NULL, the returned
string is also copied into this area and the pointer pointed to by area
is advanced.

SEE ALSO

tgoto(), tputs()

getenv(3C) in the UNIX System V Programmer's Reference Manual

[tgetent]

NAME

tgoto — Low-level *termcap* cursor-addressing function.

SYNOPSIS

```
char *tgoto(cap, column, row)
char *cap;
int column;
int row;
```

DESCRIPTION

This low-level *termcap* function substitutes the values *column* and *row* in the parameterized capability string supplied as cap. This is normally only used for absolute cursor-addressing. The string cap is the resultant string returned from tgetstr(). The string returned can then be passed to tputs() for output to the screen.

SEE ALSO

tgetstr(), tputs()

[tgoto]

NAME

tigetflag, tigetnum, tigetstr — Low-level *terminfo* entry query functions.

SYNOPSIS

```
#include <term.h>

int tigetflag(capname)
char *capname;

int tigetnum(capname)
char *capname;

char *tigetstr(capname)
char *capname;
```

DESCRIPTION

These low-level *terminfo* routines are used to query the terminfo environment. The functions assume that the internal data structures have already been filled by `setupterm()`. The argument `capname` must be a terminfo C-language variable defined in `<term.h>`.

The `tigetflag()` function returns 0 if the boolean capability is not defined for the terminal. -1 is returned if the passed argument is not a valid boolean capability.

The `tigetnum()` function returns -1 if the number capability is not defined for the terminal. -2 is returned if the passed argument is not a valid number capability.

The `tigetstr()` function returns (char *)0 if the string capability is not defined for the terminal. (char *)-1 is returned if the passed argument is not a valid string capability.

NOTE

These functions were introduced with the release of System V.

SEE ALSO

`setupterm()`, `set_curterm()`

[tigetflag]

NAME
touchline — Make it look as if the whole line has been changed.

SYNOPSIS
```
#include <curses.h>

void touchline(win, start, count)
WINDOW *win;
int start;
int count;
```

DESCRIPTION
Similar to `touchwin()`, this function touches the number of lines specified in `count` starting from line `start` within the given window `win`, effectively making it appear as though each of these lines within the window has been changed. This causes *curses* to throw away all optimization information pertaining to the specified lines within the window.

RETURNS
Void — No return value.

NOTE
This routine was introduced with the release of System V.3, although some 4BSD-based systems may support this routine with different semantics.

SEE ALSO
`touchwin()`, `touchoverlap()`

[touchline]

NAME

touchoverlap — Make it look as if overlapping regions of two windows have been changed.

SYNOPSIS

```
#include <curses.h>

void touchoverlap(win1, win2)
WINDOW *win1;
WINDOW *win2;
```

DESCRIPTION

This function touches every location within window win2 in the area which overlaps with window win1, making it appear as though the overlapping portion within win2 has been changed. This causes *curses* to throw away all optimization information pertaining to this overlapping area within the window win2.

If neither of the specified windows overlap, no changes are made.

RETURNS

Void — No return value.

NOTE

This function exists on some versions of 4BSD only, and is not a supported feature of System V.

SEE ALSO

touchwin(), touchline()

NAME

touchwin — Make it look as if the whole window has been changed.

SYNOPSIS

```
#include <curses.h>

void touchwin(win)
WINDOW *win;
```

DESCRIPTION

This function touches every location within the given window win making it appear as though the whole window has been changed. This causes *curses* to throw away all optimization information pertaining to the specified window.

This function is useful for refreshing overlapping windows.

RETURNS

Void — No return value.

SEE ALSO

touchline(), touchoverlap()

NAME

tparm — Low-level *terminfo* parameter substitution function.

SYNOPSIS

```
#include <term.h>

char *tparm(str, p1, p2, ..., p9)
char *str;
int p1, p2, ..., p9;
```

DESCRIPTION

This low-level *terminfo* routine performs runtime parameter substitution to a terminfo capability string. The argument str must be a terminfo-defined C-language variable as defined in <term.h>. The function uses up to 9 integer arguments which are used to substitute the string parameters within the passed capability string. Each argument represents a parameter within the string. For example, the *cursor_address* string capability takes two parameters: the first is the line to move to, the second is the column. Assuming that you want to move to line 10 column 5, you would do:

```
tparm(cursor_address,10,5);
```

RETURNS

tparm() returns the supplied capability string str with the parameters substituted by the specified arguments p1 to p9. The returned string can then be used as an argument to tputs(). If the supplied string contains invalid percent (%) encoded instructions, the returned string contains an error message.

NOTE

This function was introduced with the release of UNIX System V.

SEE ALSO

tputs(), putp()

terminfo(4) in the UNIX System V Programmer's Reference Manual

[tparm]

NAME

tputs, putp — Low-level *terminfo* output functions.

SYNOPSIS

```
#include <term.h>

void tputs(str, count, putc)
char *str;
int count;
int (*putc)();

void putp(str)
char *str;
```

DESCRIPTION

These low-level *terminfo* routines apply padding to the string str and then pass the string, a character at a time, to the supplied function putc() for output to the screen. The argument count specifies the amount of lines which will be affected by the padding delay. The argument putc is a user-supplied function which would typically just call the stdio macro putchar() for output to stdout.

The function putp() is provided for convenience. It calls tputs(str,count,putchar).

str must be a terminfo string variable defined in <term.h> or the returned string from either tparm(), tgetstr(), tigetstr() or tgoto().

RETURNS

Void — No return value.

SEE ALSO

stdio(3S) in the UNIX System V Programmer's Reference Manual

[tputs]

NAME

traceon, traceoff — Turn debug trace output on/off.

SYNOPSIS

```
void traceon()

void traceoff()
```

DESCRIPTION

These routines are available only to source code license sites. When compiling a *curses* program you must use the -ldcurses switch to the link loader in place of the -lcurses switch.

The function traceon() turns on debug mode, and all debug information is written to a file named "trace" in the current directory. The function traceoff() turns off debug mode and closes the trace file.

RETURNS

Void — No return value.

CAVEAT

The trace file is opened in append mode and will grow very quickly.

If the file trace cannot be opened for any reason by traceon(), then the program will exit and possibly leave the terminal in an undesirable state.

NAME

typeahead — Check for input typeahead.

SYNOPSIS

```
int typeahead(fildes)
int fildes;
```

DESCRIPTION

This function makes *curses* periodically check the keyboard input buffer
for characters while updating the screen. If characters are waiting in the
buffer and the input file descriptor `fildes` is associated with a *tty*, the
current update is suspended pending a call to `wrefresh()` or
`doupdate()`. This allows a faster response to keyboard input typed in
advance.

The argument `fildes` specifies the file descriptor to check
typeahead on; this is normally 0 (`stdin`). Typeahead can be turned off
by setting `fildes` to −1.

RETURNS

On pre-System V.3 versions of *curses*, this function has no return value.
However, on System V.3, `typeahead()` returns the value of the
previous file descriptor used for input.

NOTE

This routine was introduced with the release of System V.

SEE ALSO

flushinp()

[typeahead]

NAME

unctrl — Get a printable, string representation of a character.

SYNOPSIS

```
#include <curses.h>

unctrl(ch)
int ch;
```

DESCRIPTION

This routine is a pseudo-function defined in the file unctrl.h which is automatically included by <curses.h>. It expands the argument ch to its string representation so that the character 'Control-C', for example, is expanded to the string "^C", and the character 'z' is expanded to the string "z".

NOTE

On non-System V systems, the include file <unctrl.h> may not automatically be included by <curses.h>.

NAME

ungetch — Push key back onto *curses* input queue.

SYNOPSIS

```
void ungetch(key)
int key;
```

DESCRIPTION

This function places the key **key** back onto the *curses* input queue so that it is ready to be returned by the next call to wgetch().

The key pushed back may be any key received by wgetch() including keys which form part of the keypad.

RETURNS

Void — No return value.

NOTE

This function was introduced with the release of System V.3.

SEE ALSO

wgetch(), keypad()

NAME

vidputs, vidattr — Low-level *terminfo* functions for video attribute manipulation.

SYNOPSIS

```
#include <curses.h>

void vidputs(attrs, putc)
int attrs;
int (*putc)();

void vidattr(attrs)
int attrs;
```

DESCRIPTION

These low-level *terminfo* routines are used to control the terminal's video attributes. attrs can be any combination of video attributes as defined in the <curses.h> file. The function putc() must be supplied. This is typically a putchar(3S) like function but can be any function capable of outputting a single character.

The function vidattr() is provided for convenience and is effectively a call to vidputs(attrs,putchar).

RETURNS

Void — No return value.

NOTE

These functions were introduced with the release of UNIX System V.

SEE ALSO

tputs(), putp()

stdio(3S) in the UNIX System V Programmer's Reference Manual

[vidputs]

NAME

wnoutrefresh — Update *curses* internal virtual screen.

SYNOPSIS

```
#include <curses.h>

int wnoutrefresh(win)
WINDOW *win;
```

DESCRIPTION

This routine updates the *curses* virtual screen curscr with the contents of the window win. No actual update is done to the physical terminal screen.

RETURNS

wnoutrefresh() returns ERR if the window win is a NULL pointer. Otherwise OK is returned.

NOTE

This function was introduced with the release of System V.

SEE ALSO

doupdate(), wrefresh()

[wnoutrefresh]

Appendix
terminfo-termcap
cross-reference

The following terminfo-termcap cross-reference tables are provided for both the terminfo description designer and the C programmer. Programmers wanting to manipulate the terminal screen directly will use the low-level terminfo routines *curses* is built upon, and the information provided in these tables will be useful to them.

Within each cross-reference table the following column headings have been adopted:

Capname   The short name used to describe a capability. It is used by terminfo description writers, by C programmers using the low-level terminfo routines, and by the UNIX command **tput** which is used to query the terminfo database.

Termcap code   A two-letter code which corresponds to the old *termcap* capability name. It is used by C programmers using the *termcap emulation* routines which form part of the low-level terminfo library.

Variable   A name C programmers use to access the terminfo database via the low-level terminfo routines.

Description   A short description of its use.

A table is also provided at the back of the appendix listing termcap capabilities which are now obsolete and unsupported by terminfo.

The following indicators may appear at the end of a string capability description:

(G)   This indicates that a parameterized string is used. The string is parsed by the *terminfo* function `tparm()` with parameters as given. Parameters are numbered #n, where n specifies the nth parameter.

(*)   This indicates that padding may be proportional to the number of lines affected.

263

| TERMINFO-TERMCAP BOOLEAN FLAG CAPABILITIES ||||
Capname	Termcap code	Variable	Description
am	am	*auto_right_margin*	Terminal has automatic margins
bw	bw	*auto_left_margin*	Moving left from col 0 causes left wrap
chts	HC	*hard_cursor*	Hard-to-see cursor needs to be more visible
da	da	*memory_above*	Can retain display memory above the screen
db	db	*memory_below*	Can retain display memory below the screen
eo	eo	*erase_overstrike*	Can erase overstrikes with a blank
eslok	es	*status_line_esc_ok*	Escape can be used on the status line
gn	gn	*generic_type*	Generic line type (e.g. dialup, switch)
hc	hc	*hard_copy*	Hard-copy terminal
hs	hs	*has_status_line*	Has extra status line
hz	hz	*tilde_glitch*	Can't print tilde '˜' (such as Hazeltine)
in	in	*insert_null_glitch*	Insert mode distinguishes nulls
km	km	*has_meta_key*	Has a meta key
mc5i	5i	*prtr_silent*	Terminal aux printer causes no echo on screen
mir	mi	*move_insert_mode*	Is safe to move while in insert mode
msgr	ms	*move_standout_mode*	Is safe to move in standout modes
npc	NP	*no_pad_char*	No pad character exists for this terminal
nrrmc	NR	*non_rev_rmcup*	Smcup does not reverse rmcup
os	os	*over_strike*	Terminal overstrikes
ul	ul	*transparent_underline*	Underline character overstrikes
xenl	xn	*eat_newline_glitch*	New-line ignored after 80 cols (Concept)
xhp	xs	*ceol_standout_glitch*	Standout not erased by overwriting (hp)
xon	xo	*xon_xoff*	Terminal uses xon/xoff handshaking
xsb	xb	*no_esc_ctlc*	No escape or Ctrl-C, (f1=escape, f2=ctrl C)
xt	xt	*dest_tabs_magic_smso*	Tabs are destructive and overwrite

\multicolumn{4}{c}{TERMINFO-TERMCAP NUMERIC CAPABILITIES}
Capname	*Termcap code*	*Variable*	*Description*
cols	co	*columns*	Number of columns in a line
it	it	*init_tabs*	Tabs are initially every # spaces
lh	lh	*label_height*	Number of lines in each label (soft labels)
lines	li	*lines*	Number of lines on screen or page
lm	lm	*lines_of_memory*	Lines of memory if > lines (0=varies)
lw	lw	*label_width*	Number of columns in each label
nlab	Nl	*num_labels*	Number of labels on the screen (start at 1)
pb	pb	*padding_baud_rate*	Lowest baud rate where padding needed
wsl	ws	*width_status_line*	Number of columns in status line
xmc	sg	*magic_cookie_glitch*	Number of blank chars left by smso or rmso

TERMINFO-TERMCAP STRING CAPABILITIES			
Capname	Termcap code	Variable	Description
acsc	ac	acs_chars	Alternate character set pairs
bel	bl	bell	Audible signal (bell)
blink	mb	enter_blink_mode	Turn on blinking mode
bold	md	enter_bold_mode	Turn on bold mode (extra bright)
cbt	bt	back_tab	Back tab (move left to next tab stop)
civis	vi	cursor_invisible	Make cursor invisible
clear	cl	clear_screen	Clear screen sequence (*)
cnorm	ve	cursor_normal	Make cursor normal (undo cvvis/civis)
cr	cr	carriage_return	Carriage return sequence (*)
csr	cs	change_scroll_region	Set scrolling region to lines #1 thru #2 (G)
cub	LE	parm_left_cursor	Move cursor left #1 number of spaces (G)
cub1	le	cursor_left	Move cursor left one space
cud	DO	parm_down_cursor	Move cursor down #1 number of lines (G*)
cud1	do	cursor_down	Move down one line
cuf	RI	parm_right_cursor	Move cursor right #1 number of spaces (G*)
cuf1	nd	cursor_right	Non-destructive space (cursor right)
cup	cm	cursor_address	Move cursor to row #1 col #2 (G)
cuu	UP	parm_up_cursor	Move cursor up #1 number of lines (G*)
cuu1	up	cursor_up	Move cursor up one line
cvvis	vs	cursor_visible	Make cursor very visible (extra bright)
dch	DC	parm_dch	Delete #1 number of charcters (G*)
dch1	dc	delete_character	Delete one character (*)
dim	mh	enter_dim_mode	Turn on half-bright mode
dl	DL	parm_delete_line	Delete #1 number of lines (G*)

		TERMINFO-TERMCAP STRING CAPABILITIES	
Capname	*Termcap code*	*Variable*	*Description*
dl1	dl	*delete_line*	Delete one line (*)
dsl	ds	*dis_status_line*	Disable the status line
ech	ec	*erase_chars*	Erase #1 number of characters (G)
ed	cd	*clr_eos*	Clear from here to the end of the display (*)
el	ce	*clr_eol*	Clear from here to the end of the line
el1	cb	*clr_bol*	Clear from here to the beginning of the line
enacs	eA	*ena_acs*	Enable the alternate character set
ff	ff	*form_feed*	Hard-copy terminal page eject (*)
flash	vb	*flash_screen*	Visible bell (flash) (may not move cursor)
fsl	fs	*from_status_line*	Return from the status line
hd	hd	*down_half_line*	Move half a line down
home	ho	*cursor_home*	Home the cursor (used if no cup)
hpa	ch	*column_address*	Move to absolute column address #1 (G)
ht	ta	*tab*	Advance to the next hardware tab stop
hts	st	*set_tab*	Set tab stop in current column of every row
hu	hu	*up_half_line*	Move half a line up
ich	IC	*parm_ich*	Insert #1 number of blank characters (G*)
ich1	ic	*insert_character*	Insert one character
if	if	*init_file*	Name of /usr/lib/tabset/? initialization file
il	AL	*parm_insert_line*	Add #1 number of new blank lines (G*)
il1	al	*insert_line*	Add one new blank line (*)
ind	sf	*scroll_forward*	Scroll the text up one line
indn	SF	*parm_index*	Scroll forward #1 number of lines (G)
invis	mk	*enter_secure_mode*	Turn on invisible character mode
ip	ip	*insert_padding*	Insert pad after the character inserted (*)

TERMINFO-TERMCAP STRING CAPABILITIES			
Capname	Termcap code	Variable	Description
iprog	iP	init_prog	Path name of program for initialization
is1	i1	init_1string	Secondary terminal initialization string
is2	is	init_2string	Main terminal initialization string
is3	i3	init_3string	Secondary terminal initialization string
kBEG	&9	key_sbeg	KEY_SBEG, shifted beginning key
kCAN	&0	key_scancel	KEY_SCANCEL, shifted cancel key
kCMD	*1	key_scommand	KEY_SCOMMAND, shifted command key
kCPY	*2	key_scopy	KEY_SCOPY, shifted copy key
kCRT	*3	key_screate	KEY_SCREATE, shifted create key
kDC	*4	key_sdc	KEY_SDC, shifted delete character key
kDL	*5	key_sdl	KEY_SDL, shifted delete line key
kEND	*7	key_send	KEY_SEND, shifted end key
kEOL	*8	key_seol	KEY_SEOL, shifted clear line key
kEXT	*9	key_sexit	KEY_SEXIT, shifted exit key
kFND	*0	key_sfind	KEY_SFIND, shifted find key
kHLP	#1	key_shelp	KEY_SHELP, shifted help key
kHOM	#2	key_shome	KEY_SHOME, shifted home key
kIC	#3	key_sic	KEY_SIC, shifted input key
kLFT	#4	key_sleft	KEY_SLEFT, shifted left arrow key
kMOV	%b	key_smove	KEY_SMOVE, shifted move key
kMSG	%a	key_smessage	KEY_SMESSAGE, shifted message key
kNXT	%c	key_snext	KEY_SNEXT, shifted next key
kOPT	%d	key_soptions	KEY_SOPTIONS, shifted options key
kPRT	%f	key_sprint	KEY_SPRINT, shifted print key
kPRV	%e	key_sprevious	KEY_SPREVIOUS, shifted prev key

TERMINFO-TERMCAP STRING CAPABILITIES			
Capname	Termcap code	Variable	Description
kRDO	%g	key_sredo	KEY_SREDO, shifted redo key
kRES	%j	key_srsume	KEY_SRSUME, shifted resume key
kRIT	%i	key_sright	KEY_SRIGHT, shifted right arrow
kRPL	%h	key_sreplace	KEY_SREPLACE, shifted replace key
kSAV	!1	key_ssave	KEY_SSAVE, shifted save key
kSPD	!2	key_ssuspend	KEY_SSUSPEND, shifted suspend key
kUND	!3	key_sundo	KEY_SUNDO, shifted undo key
ka1	K1	key_a1	KEY_A1, upper left key of keypad
ka3	K3	key_a3	KEY_A3, upper right key of keypad
kb2	K2	key_b2	KEY_B2, center key of keypad
kbeg	@1	key_beg	KEY_BEG, beg(inning) key
kbs	kb	key_backspace	KEY_BACKSPACE, backspace key
kc1	K4	key_c1	KEY_C1, lower left key of keypad
kc3	K5	key_c3	KEY_C3, lower right key of keypad
kcan	@2	key_cancel	KEY_CANCEL, cancel key
kcbt	kB	key_btab	KEY_BTAB, back-tab key
kclo	@3	key_close	KEY_CLOSE, close key
kclr	kC	key_clear	KEY_CLEAR, clear screen or erase key
kcmd	@4	key_command	KEY_COMMAND, command key
kcpy	@5	key_copy	KEY_COPY, copy key
kcrt	@6	key_create	KEY_CREATE, create key
kctab	kt	key_ctab	KEY_CTAB, clear-tab key
kcub1	kl	key_left	KEY_LEFT, left arrow key
kcud1	kd	key_down	KEY_DOWN, down arrow key
kcuf1	kr	key_right	KEY_RIGHT, right arrow key

TERMINFO-TERMCAP STRING CAPABILITIES			
Capname	Termcap code	Variable	Description
kcuu1	ku	key_up	KEY_UP, up arrow key
kdch1	kD	key_dc	KEY_DC, delete character key
kdl1	kL	key_dl	KEY_DL, delete line key
ked	kS	key_eos	KEY_EOS, clear-to-end-of-screen key
kel	kE	key_eol	KEY_EOL, clear-to-end-of-line key
kend	@7	key_end	KEY_END, end key
kent	@8	key_enter	KEY_ENTER, enter/send (unreliable)
kext	@9	key_exit	KEY_EXIT, exit key
kf0	k0	key_f0	KEY_F(0), function key f0
kf1	k1	key_f1	KEY_F(1), function key f1
kf2	k2	key_f2	KEY_F(2), function key f2
kf3	k3	key_f3	KEY_F(3), function key f3
kf4	k4	key_f4	KEY_F(4), function key f4
kf5	k5	key_f5	KEY_F(5), function key f5
kf6	k6	key_f6	KEY_F(6), function key f6
kf7	k7	key_f7	KEY_F(7), function key f7
kf8	k8	key_f8	KEY_F(8), function key f8
kf9	k9	key_f9	KEY_F(9), function key f9
kf10	k;	key_f10	KEY_F(10), function key f10
kf11	F1	key_f11	KEY_F(11), function key f11
kf12	F2	key_f12	KEY_F(12), function key f12
kf13	F3	key_f13	KEY_F(13), function key f13
kf14	F4	key_f14	KEY_F(14), function key f14
kf15	F5	key_f15	KEY_F(15), function key f15
kf16	F6	key_f16	KEY_F(16), function key f16

TERMINFO-TERMCAP STRING CAPABILITIES			
Capname	*Termcap code*	*Variable*	*Description*
kf17	F7	key_f17	KEY_F(17), function key f17
kf18	F8	key_f18	KEY_F(18), function key f18
kf19	F9	key_f19	KEY_F(19), function key f19
kf20	FA	key_f20	KEY_F(20), function key f20
kf21	FB	key_f21	KEY_F(21), function key f21
kf22	FC	key_f22	KEY_F(22), function key f22
kf23	FD	key_f23	KEY_F(23), function key f23
kf24	FE	key_f24	KEY_F(24), function key f24
kf25	FF	key_f25	KEY_F(25), function key f25
kf26	FG	key_f26	KEY_F(26), function key f26
kf27	FH	key_f27	KEY_F(27), function key f27
kf28	FI	key_f28	KEY_F(28), function key f28
kf29	FJ	key_f29	KEY_F(29), function key f29
kf30	FK	key_f30	KEY_F(30), function key f30
kf31	FL	key_f31	KEY_F(31), function key f31
kf32	FM	key_f32	KEY_F(32), function key f32
kf33	FN	key_f33	KEY_F(33), function key f33
kf34	FO	key_f34	KEY_F(34), function key f34
kf35	FP	key_f35	KEY_F(35), function key f35
kf36	FQ	key_f36	KEY_F(36), function key f36
kf37	FR	key_f37	KEY_F(37), function key f37
kf38	FS	key_f38	KEY_F(38), function key f38
kf39	FT	key_f39	KEY_F(39), function key f39
kf40	FU	key_f40	KEY_F(40), function key f40
kf41	FV	key_f41	KEY_F(41), function key f41

TERMINFO-TERMCAP STRING CAPABILITIES			
Capname	Termcap code	Variable	Description
kf42	FW	key_f42	KEY_F(42), function key f42
kf43	FX	key_f43	KEY_F(43), function key f43
kf44	FY	key_f44	KEY_F(44), function key f44
kf45	FZ	key_f45	KEY_F(45), function key f45
kf46	Fa	key_f46	KEY_F(46), function key f46
kf47	Fb	key_f47	KEY_F(47), function key f47
kf48	Fc	key_f48	KEY_F(48), function key f48
kf49	Fd	key_f49	KEY_F(49), function key f49
kf50	Fe	key_f50	KEY_F(50), function key f50
kf51	Ff	key_f51	KEY_F(51), function key f51
kf52	Fg	key_f52	KEY_F(52), function key f52
kf53	Fh	key_f53	KEY_F(53), function key f53
kf54	Fi	key_f54	KEY_F(54), function key f54
kf55	Fj	key_f55	KEY_F(55), function key f55
kf56	Fk	key_f56	KEY_F(56), function key f56
kf57	Fl	key_f57	KEY_F(57), function key f57
kf58	Fm	key_f58	KEY_F(58), function key f58
kf59	Fn	key_f59	KEY_F(59), function key f59
kf60	Fo	key_f60	KEY_F(60), function key f60
kf61	Fp	key_f61	KEY_F(61), function key f61
kf62	Fq	key_f62	KEY_F(62), function key f62
kf63	Fr	key_f63	KEY_F(63), function key f63
kfnd	@0	key_find	KEY_FIND, find key
khlp	%1	key_help	KEY_HELP, help key
khome	kh	key_home	KEY_HOME, home key

TERMINFO-TERMCAP STRING CAPABILITIES			
Capname	Termcap code	Variable	Description
khts	kT	key_stab	KEY_STAB, set-tab key
kich1	kI	key_ic	KEY_IC, insert char/enter insert mode key
kil1	kA	key_il	KEY_IL, insert line key
kind	kF	key_sf	KEY_SF, scroll-forward/down key
kll	kH	key_ll	KEY_LL, home-down key
kmov	%4	key_move	KEY_MOVE, move key
kmrk	%2	key_mark	KEY_MARK, mark key
kmsg	%3	key_message	KEY_MESSAGE, message key
knp	kN	key_npage	KEY_NPAGE, next-page/page-down key
knxt	%5	key_next	KEY_NEXT, next object key
kopn	%6	key_open	KEY_OPEN, open key
kopt	%7	key_options	KEY_OPTIONS, options key
kpp	kP	key_ppage	KEY_PPAGE, previous-page/page-up key
kprt	%9	key_print	KEY_PRINT, print or copy key
kprv	%8	key_previous	KEY_PREVIOUS, previous object key
krdo	%0	key_redo	KEY_REDO, redo key
kref	&1	key_reference	KEY_REFERENCE, reference key
kres	&5	key_resume	KEY_RESUME, resume key
krfr	&2	key_refresh	KEY_REFRESH, refresh key
kri	kR	key_sr	KEY_SR, scroll-backward/up key
krmir	kM	key_eic	KEY_EIC, exit insert mode key
krpl	&3	key_replace	KEY_REPLACE, replace key
krst	&4	key_restart	KEY_RESTART, restart key
ksav	&6	key_save	KEY_SAVE, save key
kslt	*6	key_select	KEY_SELECT, select key
kspd	&7	key_suspend	KEY_SUSPEND, suspend key

TERMINFO-TERMCAP STRING CAPABILITIES			
Capname	*Termcap code*	*Variable*	*Description*
ktbc	ka	*key_catab*	KEY_CATAB, clear-all-tabs key
kund	&8	*key_undo*	KEY_UNDO, undo key
lf0	l0	*lab_f0*	Labels on function key f0 if not f0
lf1	l1	*lab_f1*	Labels on function key f1 if not f1
lf2	l2	*lab_f2*	Labels on function key f2 if not f2
lf3	l3	*lab_f3*	Labels on function key f3 if not f3
lf4	l4	*lab_f4*	Labels on function key f4 if not f4
lf5	l5	*lab_f5*	Labels on function key f5 if not f5
lf6	l6	*lab_f6*	Labels on function key f6 if not f6
lf7	l7	*lab_f7*	Labels on function key f7 if not f7
lf8	l8	*lab_f8*	Labels on function key f8 if not f8
lf9	l9	*lab_f9*	Labels on function key f9 if not f9
lf10	la	*lab_f10*	Labels on function key f10 if not f10
ll	ll	*cursor_to_ll*	Last line, first column (if no cup)
mc0	ps	*print_screen*	Print contents of the screen
mc4	pf	*prtr_off*	Turn the printer off
mc5	po	*prtr_on*	Turn the printer on
mc5p	p0	*prtr_non*	Turn the printer on for #1 number of bytes
mgc	MC	*clear_margins*	Clear left and right soft margins
mrcup	CM	*cursor_mem_address*	Memory relative cursor-addressing
nel	nw	*newline*	New-line (behaves like cr followed by lf)
pad	pc	*pad_char*	Pad character other than NULL
pfkey	pk	*pkey_key*	Program funct key #1 to type string #2
pfloc	pl	*pkey_local*	Program funct key #1 to execute string #2
pfx	px	*pkey_xmit*	Program funct key #1 to transmit string #2

		TERMINFO-TERMCAP STRING CAPABILITIES	
Capname	*Termcap code*	*Variable*	*Description*
pln	pn	*plab_norm*	Program label #1 to show string #2
prot	mp	*enter_protected_mode*	Turn on protected mode
rc	rc	*restore_cursor*	Restore cursor to last saved position
rep	rp	*repeat_char*	Character #1 is repeated #2 times (G*)
rev	mr	*enter_reverse_mode*	Turn on reverse video mode
rf	rf	*reset_file*	Name of file containing reset string
ri	sr	*scroll_reverse*	Scroll text down one line
rin	SR	*parm_rindex*	Scroll backward #1 number of lines (G)
rmacs	ae	*exit_alt_charset_mode*	End alternate character set mode
rmam	RA	*exit_am_mode*	Turn off automatic margins
rmcup	te	*exit_ca_mode*	String to end programs that use cup
rmdc	ed	*exit_delete_mode*	End delete mode
rmir	ei	*exit_insert_mode*	End insert mode
rmkx	ke	*keypad_local*	End keypad-transmit mode
rmln	LF	*label_off*	Turn off soft labels
rmm	mo	*meta_off*	Turn off meta mode
rmp	rP	*char_padding*	Character padding time if not in insert mode
rmso	se	*exit_standout_mode*	End standout mode
rmul	ue	*exit_underline_mode*	End underscore mode
rmxon	RX	*exit_xon_mode*	Turn off xon/xoff handshaking
rs1	r1	*reset_1string*	Reset terminal completely to sane modes
rs2	r2	*reset_2string*	Reset terminal completely to sane modes
rs3	r3	*reset_3string*	Reset terminal completely to sane modes
sc	sc	*save_cursor*	Save current cursor position

TERMINFO-TERMCAP STRING CAPABILITIES			
Capname	Termcap code	Variable	Description
sgr	sa	set_attributes	Define the video attributes (G9)
sgr0	me	exit_attribute_mode	Turn off all attributes
smacs	as	enter_alt_charset_mode	Enter alternate character set mode
smam	SA	enter_am_mode	Turn on automatic margins
smcup	ti	enter_ca_mode	String to begin programs that use cup
smdc	dm	enter_delete_mode	Enter delete mode
smgl	ML	set_left_margin	Set soft left margin
smgr	MR	set_right_margin	Set soft right margin
smir	im	enter_insert_mode	Enter insert mode
smkx	ks	keypad_xmit	Start keypad-transmit mode
smln	LO	label_on	Turn on soft labels
smm	mm	meta_on	Turn on 8-bit meta mode
smso	so	enter_standout_mode	Begin standout mode
smul	us	enter_underline_mode	Start underscore mode
smxon	SX	enter_xon_mode	Turn on xon/xoff handshaking
tbc	ct	clear_all_tabs	Clear all tab stops
tsl	ts	to_status_line	Move column number #1 in status line
uc	uc	underline_char	Underscore one character and move past it
vpa	cv	row_address	Move to absolute line address #1 (G)
wind	wi	set_window	Current window is lines #1-#2 cols #3-#4
xoffc	XF	xoff_character	X-off character
xonc	XN	xon_character	X-on character

OBSOLETE TERMCAP CAPABILITIES		
Termcap code	Type of Capability	Description
bc	string	Backspace sequence (default is ^H — use cub1)
bs	boolean	Terminal uses ^H for backspace
dB	numeric	Backspace delay for hard-copy devices (milliseconds)
dC	numeric	Carriage-return delay for hard-copy devices (milliseconds)
dF	numeric	Formfeed delay for hard-copy devices (milliseconds)
dN	numeric	New-line delay for hard-copy devices (milliseconds)
dT	numeric	Tab delay for hard-copy devices (milliseconds)
dV	numeric	Vertical tab delay for hard-copy devices (milliseconds)
EP	boolean	Terminal uses Even Parity
HD	boolean	Terminal operates in Half Duplex
ko	string	List of alternate termcap capabilities which map to oddly named special keys (comma separated)
LC	string	Turn on lower-case mode
ma	string	Sequence to map keypad keys to cursor movement keys — needed for *vi* version 2
ml	string	Lock memory above the cursor
mu	string	Unlock memory above cursor (reverse of ml)
NL	boolean	Terminal uses line-feed for new-line (\n)
nc	boolean	Carriage-return glitch (does not work properly)
nl	string	Character used for new-line if not ^J
ns	boolean	Terminal scrolls abnormally
OP	boolean	Terminal uses Odd Parity
pt	boolean	Terminal supports hardware-tabs
rs	string	Reset the terminal to a sane operating mode
UC	string	Turn on upper-case mode
xr	boolean	Return character causes the line to be cleared
xx	boolean	Line insert does not work properly (Tektronix 4025)

Index